"*Road Rules* is a critical tool for navigating through life. Andrew J. Sherman is one of the rare ones who has seen the world from inside out and outside in. He has walked the road, driven the road, helped those who were its victims find new ways to succeed, advised those who were its winners identify and implement new ways to climb the heights. Andrew's latest book is not a "good read," it is an "essential read." I plan to read it again and again. Why? Because it did the most valuable thing for me: helped me to see what I thought I already knew in a new light and from a fresh perspective."

Mark Stevens
CEO, MSCO and Author of the Best Selling Books
God Is A Salesman *and* Your Marketing Sucks!

"This is the handbook I wish I would have had at 16. It would have made the ride of life much smoother! *Road Rules* gives us all a navigational guide to the values that we all embrace but don't always follow. Fasten your seatbelts!"

Dara Feldman
Director of Educational Initiatives
Virtues Project International

"I can't think of anyone who knows how to squeeze more juice out of 24 hours of a life than Andrew Sherman! His grasp of what drives and motivates people is unparalleled. If anyone is qualified to teach us about what makes for a successful *Road Rules* experience, it's Andrew!"

Margarita Rozenfeld
Chief Visionary
YES! Circle

"Andrew J. Sherman's books should be required reading for every person who dreams big dreams and wants to turn them into reality. *Road Rules* is equal parts motivation, inspiration and practical, hands-on advice for staying on track in life. I could not put it down once I started reading this highly enjoyable book. My advice: Start reading Road Rules TODAY!"

Brian Moran
President
Moran Media Group

"*Road Rules: Be the Truck. Not the Squirrel* is packed with keen insights and suffused with realism and practicality. Andrew Sherman provides a crisp, compelling, eye-opening narrative that that transforms seeming imperatives into options and choices. While you might want to spend Tuesdays with Morrie, you will want to spend each day reading from this collection of wisdom. Sherman moves seamlessly between classical thought and popular culture. This "how to" book for daily life is not to be missed."

Andrew F. Popper
Professor of Law and author of Bordering on
Madness; An American Land Use Tale

"*Road Rules* is a work of art. It is chock a block full of insightful, inspiring and appropriate information. I love the fact that there is an inspirational and explanatory piece for everybody. Thanks for sharing this great piece of your inner being with us all. It helps us all to 'Keep On Truckin'. "

John "Pappy" Papaloukas
President, Villages Pizza and Overall Really Nice Guy

"Life's true road to happiness is never straight. Andrew J. Sherman's *Road Rules* provides a memorable analogy for navigating the journey."

Verne Harnish
Founder of EO and CEO of Gazelles, Author
of Mastering the Rockefeller Habits

"Andrew J Sherman's *Road Rules* is a 'great GPS for life'. He covers life ups and downs, and everything in between. A book that has you think, reflect and enjoy. There is definitely something for everyone on this Journey!"

Keith Alper
CEO/Executive Producer, Creative Producers Group

"Observing life from the driver's seat, Andrew J. Sherman has discovered dozens of metaphors, from the wise to the whacked in *Road Rules*. How do you measure your life's progress--with a speedometer, tachometer or odometer? Why do so many accidents occur in the hour light and darkness? If you had a "How's My Driving?" sticker on your backside, what would people call into your 800 number? There's plenty of muse over as you motor along. And you've got to love a book that can invoke, on a single page, the wisdom of Bruce Springsteen, Swiss philosopher Henri Amiel and the guy who invented the infinitely adjustable windshield wiper."

Craig Stoltz
Former Editor of the Washington Post *and Web 2.0 Guru*

"Knowing Andrew as I do over many years and many miles, I can tell you that *Road Rules* is suffused with the true spirit and passion of his authentic, relentless drive to educate and inspire. Every page offers some bit of wisdom that resonates in a powerful way with our everyday experience. This is a book you will want to read once a year and give copies to your children."

John Hrastar
CEO InterSource and Radio Show Host, The Business Destiny Show

"*Road Rules* helped me create some order out of chaos created by the random thoughts that we all have about the meaning of life. The insights in this great book helped me look at many things from a wholly different perspective. Thanks for helping me learn how to truly be the truck and not the squirrel."

Jeff Van Sloan
Senior Vice President, Owens Corning Corporation

"Andrew's analogies to driving experiences in *Road Rules* crystallizes his points about life with precision and humor for a truly rewarding and enjoyable read. He appears to have another winning book on his hands and definitely worth a look (whenever you are not driving!) !"

Barbara Weltman
Host, Build Your Business Radio Show
www.BarbaraWeltman.com

"In *Road Rules*, Andrew J. Sherman uses an interesting analogy – driving along the road of life – to make a variety of impactful insights. If you're like me, you'll find yourself wanting to reread this book to refresh and recall those insights. The book definitely accomplished its purpose: to help me travel my own life's road a little wiser. One good thought followed by another, over and over again. Even when Sherman writes something you already know, he makes it clearer, simpler, and more relevant to your life. You'll find yourself nodding "yes" throughout this book. I had two reactions after reading this book: (1) I want to read it again; and (2) I'm already planning to reread once a year for the rest of my life."

Arthur A. Bushkin
Chairman & CEO
Stargazer Foundation

"For over 20 years those of us in the business world have been privileged to receive Andrew Sherman's wisdom, experience and insights through his articles, books and talks. Now the rest of the world will experience the same in his fabulous new book: *Road Rules*. A book you will start and want to drive through to the end in one sitting. This little book is destined to become a bestseller as it's practical wisdom applies to every facet of your life."

Andrew Szabo
The Marketing Chef
Author of Foundations to Irresistible Marketing

"Andrew J. Sherman has been a friend and trusted advisor for over 15 years. As Tom Cochrane says, "Life is a Highway"... Andrew's *Road Rules* provides a much welcome road map to navigate life's complicated and challenging highway. I would recommend it for anyone and everyone! "

Jeff Dennis
Serial Entrepreneur and co-author of Lessons from the Edge:
Survival Skills for Starting *and* Growing a Company

"*Road Rules* is a winner at the checkered flag! Andrew J. Sherman does it again! Known for taking legal and business topics and making them easy to understand and profit by, Andrew now takes us by the hand and tackles the bigger issues of life. A great road map, and a must read for anyone at any age!

JW Dicks
Best Selling Author, Entrepreneur and Attorney

"For many years, Andrew J. Sherman has taught us how to achieve two primary elements of business success: excellence in growth and financial competence. With his latest work, *Road Rules*, he completes the 'hat trick' of true success by sharing his wisdom on what is surely the most important issue of the 21st century: our connection to each other. Thanks, Andrew. We really needed this book, now and forever."

Jim Blasingame
Leading small business expert, award-winning host of
The Small Business Advocate Show and Author of titles Small
Business Is Like A Bunch Of Bananas
and Three Minutes To Success.

"Andrew J. Sherman has the insight of a brilliant philosopher who has taken what he learned from navigating the worlds of life, law and business and applies them to our everyday challenges and opportunities. He offers meaningful lessons and deep insights which help us learn, share, grow, and prosper in all aspects of our lives. Andrew's insight stays with you because it's not only real, but it is presented in a concentrated and enjoyable format that stimulates your thinking."

Sue Hesse
Entrepreneur-in-Residence and Senior Program Consultant,
Ewing Marion Kauffman Foundation and former International
President of the Young Entrepreneurs Organization (YEO)

"Andrew J. Sherman's *Road Rules* is a great book filled with insights for both early stage as well as seasoned entrepreneurs alike, but within its covers include life lessons for all of us. Two thumbs way up!"

Cliff Michaels
CEO/Founder/Author
One Day MBA Success Courses on Demand
Past President, Young Entrepreneurs' Organization Los Angeles

"What a great road trip!! Only Andrew J. Sherman can be a tour guide on the most tortuous part of our daily existence and turn it into a road map for life insights and success. *Road Rules* offers not only key lessons about life through our daily commute, but encourages us to look for the hidden meaning and wisdom in all our our seemingly mundane experiences and activities."

Karen Kerrigan
President & CEO, Small Business & Entrepreneurship
Council and the Women Entrepreneurs (WE) Council
and Co-Founder, Growth Without Barriers

"Yet again Andrew J. Sherman has written a powerful yet simple book that brings understanding to some key issues that affect our business and personal lives. *Road Rules* is a fantastic book that gives the reader some straightforward rules to help navigate the road of life. My particular favorite is "Be the Truck, not the Squirrel". We all spend our days dealing with business and personal challenges and decisions that have enormous impact on our lives and the lives of the people around us. We as business leaders have to make decisions on a daily basis that will impact those around us and having a book like *Road Rules* gives the questions and frameworks to help ensure we are asking the right questions of ourselves to make better decisions. Andrew has given us a compass to be better leaders and family members if we digest his navigating system and push on the gas and step on the brakes appropriately. Thank you Andrew....we needed that fuel for our engines!"

Douglas K. Mellinger
Vice Chairman & Founder
Foundation Source

"Andrew J. Sherman takes great delight in teaching and inspiring through analogies that permit us to instantly draw on our experiences and understand that the meaning of life's journey is indeed often found on the road not taken. Whether speeding to meet our destiny or finding ourselves stuck in the slow lane as others seem to whisk by, *Road Rules* will show you that being a great driver of your own life can be found in this wonderful read!"

Cynthia de Lorenzi
Founder, Success in the Ciry

"Many authors communicate with metaphors while others illustrate with real world examples. Andrew J. Sherman's book *Road Rules* marries these two worlds in a way that you will get it …and when you get it , you've got it for life. A must read for anyone interested in a smoother journey down the road of life."

Mark Richardson
President of Case and Author of How Fit is your Business?

"The road to success is a treacherous one. The journey is fraught with many rules, signs, detours, potholes, and traffic. Andrew J. Sherman's *Road Rules* is a guide to navigating through these challenges and risks with direction, purpose and inner meaning so that you can get to your destination safely and soundly."

S. Tien Wong
Philanthropist, Serial Entrepreneur and Chairman
Opus 8 Fund

"What starts as a catchy title evolves into different look at life's journey that can change your perspectives and your pathway as the pages of *Road Rules* unfolds...a must read!"

Jason Stern
Publisher and CEO
Braddock Communications, Inc.

"If there is anything I have learned over the decades about Andrew J. Sherman is that his true life's mission and purpose is to teach, as he is one of the great educators of our time. In this soon to be landmark book, *Road Rules* provides you not only with the needed roadmap, but more importantly gets you to think about the most important things in life and therefore living the life you deserve. Once you start reading this book you will not want to put it down, especially those who are at a real crossroad or crowded intersection in their journey. I am so thankful that Andrew took his own advice and wrote this book, as his keen insights, incredible wisdom and lessons on life are priceless. He is a true Bodhisattva that I am so thankful to be able to call my dear friend".

Mitchell Schlimer
Serial entrepreneur, CEO of the Let's Talk Business Network®
(www.ltbn.com); Voice of national radio show "Let's Talk Business" ; developing "Entrepreneur Hall Of Fame & Museum" (www.theehalloffame.com).

"This is Andrew J. Sherman's best work by far. Reading *Road Rules* was a sheer joy with the feeling of driving at 150 mph on the Autobahn. Mr. Sherman has pulled out the essence of life, its trials and tribulations, and simplified strategies to bring out the best in one's life to simple, easy-to-relate to "rules". A great book for everyone to extract the best life has to offer by remembering and following simple rules.

Shiv Krishnan
Chairman & CEO
INDUS Corporation

"The traditional rules of career, business and life, that have governed our actions for so long, have fundamentally changed. Everyone knows it and the resulting anxiety has created a paralysis that has stifled individual growth and development. Now, fortunately, comes Andrew J. Sherman and *Road Rules*. Andrew had provided a clear blueprint for life and success in the new world order. It is a blueprint not drawn simply from the halls of academia but from Andrew's remarkable lifetime of success."

Joe Watson
Nationally recognized thought leader on diversity in
the workplace and author of Without Excuses

"Given the recent financial crisis in our country, every American needs to read *Road Rules*! We need to get back to our core values and principles that guide us to make the right long term decisions, as Andrew so brilliantly demonstrates in this book. It has become increasingly hard to do the "right thing" because of societal pressures, distractions, and temptations. Andrew's opening quote is invaluable: "Let me not swerve from my life's true path, for it is on this road that my soul connects to its divine source." His book will provide you the sense of peace that we are all very hungry for given the increasing complexity of our daily lives."

Terry Thorson Cox
President & CEO
Business Innovation & Growth (BIG) supported by Inc. Magazine
ThinkBIG!

ROAD RULES

BE THE TRUCK.
NOT THE SQUIRREL.

ROAD RULES

BE THE TRUCK.
NOT THE SQUIRREL.

ANDREW J. SHERMAN

Published by Elevate, Charleston, South Carolina.
Member of Advantage Media Group.

ELEVATE is a registered trademark and the
Elevate colophon is a trademark of Advantage Media Group, Inc.

Printed in the United States of America

ISBN: 978-1-60194-021-6

Library of Congress Cataloging-in-Publication Data

Sherman, Andrew J.
Road rules-- be the truck, not the squirrel : learn the 12 essential rules for navigating the road of life / by Andrew J. Sherman.
p. cm.
Includes bibliographical references and index.
ISBN 978-1-60194-021-6 (alk. paper)
1. Success. 2. Conduct of life. 3. Automobile driving--Miscellanea. I. Title.
BJ1611.2.S48 2008
158--dc22
                                        2008023163

"Let Me Not Swerve From My Life's True Path,
For It Is On This Road That My Soul Connects To
Its Divine Source"

-- ***Andrew J. Sherman***

For all of you that have helped others
travel confidently towards their destination.

ACKNOWLEDGEMENTS

It is virtually impossible to formally thank and acknowledge all who have helped me along the road of life. I am blessed with the fact that there are many and I have tried hard to return the favor. As I thought through the process of who to praise, I realized that all of us should build a Wall of Gratitude in our lives. Grab a pen or a keyboard and write down the 10, 25 or even 50 people since your school days who have helped you in your travels. For many of us, the list is hundreds or even thousands, but can we recall their names, their faces and their good deeds? Are you able to make a similar list of the lives you have helped and the paths which you have enriched? It is my hope and prayer that by reading the words that lay ahead of you in this book, that you will realize and embrace the importance of this exercise.

Turning to the names that have specifically contributed to this manuscript becoming a reality, my executive assistant, Jo Lynch, who once again deserves the credit for turning my chicken scratch into prose. The team at Advantage Media Group, namely Adam Witty, Kevin Mulvaney, John Myers and Alison Morse, have kept me on task and on schedule as an idea turned into a book that we can all be proud of. When the manuscript needed one more round of truly professional and insightful editing, I turned to my long-time friend and journalist, Elaine Pofeldt. I would be nowhere without the love and support of my family and particularly my wife and lifelong travel partner, Judy, and our two amazing children, Matthew and Jennifer.

And finally, I want to acknowledge and thank all of you, the readers of *Road Rules*®. Without you, the highway of life would be very lonely.

PREFACE

Most of us don't consider our daily commute or a drive to the mall very enlightening. We are more likely to suffer boredom, road rage, frustration, or even a fender bender than to embrace life's most meaningful lessons. But what if I told you that virtually everything you needed to know about navigating the road of life could be learned during a routine errand run, behind the comfort of your steering wheel?

So many of our core life lessons are reinforced by the simple act of driving a vehicle:

- ⊙ when to speed up and when to slow down

- ⊙ when to yield and when to come to a complete stop

- ⊙ when to add gas and when to add oil

- ⊙ when to allow another to pass you by and when to make your move

- ⊙ when to proceed with caution because children are playing or there is construction ahead

- ⊙ when to give your keys to a friend to avoid driving under the influence of drugs or alcohol

- ⊙ when and how to communicate when it is not clear who has the right of way

The lessons that we learn on the road that get us to our destination are in fact the same lessons that we need to understand to achieve our goals in life. The rules that we must follow to maintain our driver's licenses—our privilege of sharing the road with others—are the same rules we need to embrace to lead an enlightened and productive life.

THE SPONGE AND THE TELESCOPE

Road Rules is the book that was destined not to be written.

After writing 17 books about the dynamics of business growth, delivering hundreds of lectures and speeches on expansion strategies and serving as an advisor to thousands of entrepreneurs and more established companies, I wanted to share some insights and observations that might be of interest to a broader audience. The challenges in building a company are the same challenges that we all face in building our lives – the need to establish trust and confidence, the need for crystal clear communication, the need for having a game plan and a road map for your journey, the need to maintain healthy and effective relationships, the need to harvest our intellectual assets, the need to bond with coaches, advisors and mentors, the need to have systems to measure our progress – all of these are inextricably intertwined in our personal and professional lives.

In 25 years of serving as a lawyer, a sounding board and strategic advisor, I have seen no greater inflection point than today when the path to growing companies and the path to a fulfilled personal and spiritual journey are at an intersection. The aggregate of the events of September 11, 2001, the violations of trust leading to Sarbanes-Oxley, the challenges to peace and harmony around the world, the rising costs of energy and the impact of technology have lead us all to be intensely focused on the achievement of smooth passage down the road of life. We are also re-examining our definition of words like goodness, integrity, respect and values. We want to lead an enriched and purposeful life, but are not always clear as to which road to travel or the navigational rules to arrive at our target destinations. We want to align and reconcile our approaches to our personal lives with the strategies deployed in our professional lives and career paths. We strive for integration and consistency of the values we embrace in our homes with the values that are expected of us in the workplace. It is an issue bigger than morals, ethics, leadership or good personal or organizational governance – it begins with a basic commitment to being better and more considerate of others as drivers on the road of life.

And so I began my journey to publish my thoughts, observations and insights on navigating the road of life. The reaction was uniform – "hey, that sounds great, but you are a business book author, why don't you stick to your knitting? I am sure we can shape and bend those thoughts into lessons for business leaders." I resisted – <u>been</u> <u>there</u> and <u>done</u> <u>that</u>. And yes, they are right, there will be a *Road Rules* for entrepreneurs and growing company leaders at some point, but that was beside the point. More important to me was the need to share, the need to teach, the need to understand the linkages between building a business and building a life.

So I finally decided to publish the flagship version of *Road Rules*. In an age of self-expression empowered by Facebook, MySpace, YouTube and hundreds of other sites, self-publishing seemed like a logical way to put the words of my inner voice down on paper. Like the sponge that needs to empty its contents from time to time in order to remain productive, I needed to publish these life lessons at a time when everyone is looking for a telescope to have a better view of the road that lies ahead.

My hope and my prayer is that you take away one insight, one golden nugget of wisdom, one driving tip that you will find useful as you navigate the road of life. More than one, even better still. For when it is on that point of the highway of existence that you realize that the purpose of life is to learn to share the rules of the road with others, that is when you have truly arrived at your destination.

Road Rules® was written to provide insights into the process of transforming what we know to be the best practices and habits of safe and purposeful driving into living a meaningful and goal-driven life - one devoted to helping others, to helping ourselves, and to achieving your professional, financial and wealth goals. My goal is to help you look at things just a bit differently and to solve problems just a bit more creatively. Sometimes adjusting the compass dial only a few degrees in one direction or another can put you on a much more efficient path and be the key to survival and prosperity.

EVERY DAY IS A NEW DRIVING LESSON

Think back to your first driving lesson. You took your place behind the wheel, learning the critical difference of when to accelerate and when to brake. You learned how to drive a straight and focused path and the importance of taking into account the actions of others around you. The excitement of hearing the engine for the first time when you started the car was offset only by the fear of hitting something or someone and causing damage. So many aspects of the basic steps in driving a vehicle also parallel many of life's more critical lessons—which are all wrapped up in an activity that most of us take for granted and without giving it a second thought. We seem to have lost sight of our ability to find joy and excitement from the simple act of driving. You are traveling just inches above the road at 65 mph on an open stretch of road on a beautiful day! Let's learn to reconnect with the happiness to be found in the simple things in life that make our quest for the more complex easier to handle.

As you begin to embrace the premise that every day is a new driving lesson, you will become more focused on the hundreds of choices that you make from dawn to dust and that you must live with the expected and unexpected consequences of each decision. These decisions include:

- How you drive?

- What you drive?

- Where you will drive?

- At what speed will you drive?

- Who will be your passenger(s)?

- How considerate will you be to others trying to reach their destination?

And many, many others. Accountability is the lynchpin of your credibility. And integrity must make up the core of your driving record.

INTRODUCTION

DRIVING LESSONS FROM THE BODHISATTVA

"The road to triumph is paved with the
gravel of adversity, pain, and conflict."
—Naso

For many of us, how we drive today is guided by the driving styles and philosophies of our coaches, parents, and mentors. We admire their teachings and their accomplishments and we model our lives and establish our goals accordingly. Or if they were negative influence, we promise ourselves to travel a different path. Who were your driving instructors? How have their good and bad habits influenced your choices in life?

If you could turn back the hands of time, would you have chosen different driving instructors? How effective would they have been at providing you with the guidance you need on the highways, the city streets, and the winding mountain roads known as life? Were you taught to drive on all types of roads and in all types of weather conditions?

My actual driving instructor was a gentleman from West Philadelphia named Mr. Harmon. He was a large and quiet man whose look of disappointment when you pulled on the right hand turn signal to make a left turn was enough to inspire you to learn quickly and effectively. Mr. Harmon was also a bar mitzvah tutor, which taught me my first lesson in cross-selling and vertical integration – capture a kid at 12 who is nervous about his first big test in life and build his trust – then hit him again three years later for their next biggest test in life! Mr. Harmon dedicated his life to teaching the art of reading Torah and the science of parallel parking and as such, he qualified as a <u>Bodhisattva</u> – a Buddhist term which means "one who has dedicated his life to the enlightenment of others."

Are you a Bodhisattva? Have you dedicated yourself to a path of lifelong teaching <u>and</u> lifelong learning? Above the entrance way of my high school, a sign read "Enter to Learn, Go Forth to Serve." Passing through those doors every day made a permanent impression on me.

One of the central themes of *Road Rules*® is that it is never, ever too late to change your driving instructor, your driving style, the vehicle that you will drive, the passengers or cargo you carry, the road you are on, or the path you will take. You are in control of shaping your own destiny: you have the power, the tools, the resources, and the energy to influence and to change some or all of these life-defining variables as you plan and progress on your journey. ***You are the author of your own life's story.***

As Rabbi William Rudolph said, "You are not the prisoner of your past, but rather you are the architect of your future." I recognize and acknowledge that this is no easy task. Pulling yourself off a path that is destructive, unproductive, or unfulfilling can be the hardest thing that you will ever do, but is a critical step towards living an enlightened and enjoyable existence. Many hurdles may stand in your way. In the Oasis hit song, "Wonderwall," the lyric "all the roads we have to walk are winding … and all the lights that lead us there are blinding …" means that you are going to need a good navigational device and an even better pair of sunglasses! Part of this process will entail the undertaking of a "reality audit" of your existence as a driver on the road of life.

Understand the difference between <u>who</u> you are <u>vs.</u> <u>what</u> you do as you travel down the road of life. We tend to define ourselves by our job titles instead of who we really are as a person, our values and our beliefs. Understand the difference between what <u>gives</u> you energy <u>vs.</u> what <u>takes</u> your energy away. ***We spend most of our lives devoted to activities that diminish our fuel and then wonder why our tank is empty.***

Can we change? Are we capable of becoming different types of drivers if that is what it takes to get on the right path or to drive in a different style? Some say not. In his book, *Go Put Your Strengths To Work*, Marcus Buckingham posits that we cannot change our personalities. In fact, as we mature, he says, we become even more of who we already are. Buckingham argues that we are incapable of transforming ourselves into the person we have always wanted to be. In a society that regularly allows and empowers us to reinvent ourselves, I am not so sure that I agree. But he does have a very important lesson for us all: find your true inner strengths and build on them to grow as a person. Buckingham argues that our values, skills, behaviors, and levels of self-awareness will evolve, but since the dominant aspects of our personality instilled since birth will remain the same, we must seek to grow in the areas of our greatest strengths. When we seek to expedite our travels on the journey of life by driving in our innate style, we will be the most inquisitive, the most resilient, the most creative, and the most open to learning. We must take the time to get in touch with our inner strengths in order to channel them into the most productive pathways as we mature as drivers.

For those of you reading this book that are resistant to (or fear) change, this should come as comfort food for the brain. Strive to be more directly in touch with who and what type of driver you really are and always have been to find your inner strengths and plot your course accordingly. A journey of a thousand miles begins with your keys in the ignition and your foot on the accelerator. Fire up your engine and move yourself forward. As a lifelong pragmatist, I am not as concerned with whether a desire to change or a desire to be more of what you already are is your motivation, as long as you commit to establish goals, get off the couch, and begin traveling righteously towards your destination. As Benjamin Mays said, "The tragedy of life doesn't lie in not reaching your goals. The tragedy lies in having no goals to reach."

Regardless of your views as to how we evolve as drivers on the road of life, momentum and progress are critical. You cannot remain stagnant. Will Rogers once said, "Even if you are on the right track, you are going to get run over if you just sit there." Good advice from a guy who rode horses—it sounds more like it would have come from a NASCAR® driver.

Most of the successful people that I have met in my life are never satisfied with their destination. They are always striving to reach new heights and travel to new places and levels of accomplishment. Momentum is critical for their progress along the highway of life. They rarely pause at a rest stop to over celebrate their success and are constantly mapping out new journeys – they live their lives for the purpose of explaining uncharted highways. They know that perfection is illusive – there is always room for improvement, for better approaches, for new learning. They also understand and embrace the fact that there will be challenges and adversity along the way, but do not allow these speed bumps to interrupt their momentum.

I have had the pleasure and honor of meeting Mayor Sam Sullivan several times while visiting Vancouver on business trips. Mayor Sullivan is a quadriplegic and is one of the only wheelchair-defined Mayors in the world. His commitment to community service, his smile, the passion behind his words are a reminder to all of us that great drivers and teachers present themselves in many forms and in many different (and often unexpected) places. Next time you have traveled a bit off the right path, find the video online of Mayor Sullivan doing "figure eights" in his chair while carrying the Olympic Flag at the closing ceremony of the 2006 Olympic Winter Games in Torino. If watching this video clip does not make your heart sing, then you better have your pulse checked.

Our increasingly technological society has put a premium on not only *what* you know, but also on your *willingness to learn.* Your ability to absorb, process, and apply knowledge has become as critical than the underlying knowledge itself. Our fast-paced and ever-changing world, shaped by a constantly evolving Internet and other powerful search tools has leveled the playing field on *access* to information, so the value-added is on the creativity and strategy you can formulate from this knowledge base. We must focus on teaching the next generation (and ourselves) *how* to learn, not *what* to learn, because the "what" is likely to become stale or unusable within a short period of time, but the "how" provides a set of skills for lifelong use.

It is also critical to develop a "liver and kidney" function for your brain – that which will filter out the information which is helpful and good from that which is clutter or harmful. Without this filter in place, your brain becomes like an oversaturated sponge, which is heavy and dysfunctional. The distinction between what will be useful as tools for your journey and what is just dead weight is determined by your experiences, your goals and your ability to sharply focus on reaching your destination. Lao Tzu, a Chinese philosopher, once wrote: "In the pursuit of knowledge, every day something is acquired. In the pursuit of wisdom, every day something is dropped."

RULES FOR BEING HUMAN (AUTHOR UNKNOWN)

You will receive a body. You may like it or hate it, but it will be yours for as long as you live. How you take care of it or fail to take care of it can make an enormous difference in your daily life.

You will learn lessons. You are enrolled in a full-time school called Life. Each day, you will be presented with opportunities to learn what you need to know. The lessons presented are often completely different from those you THINK you need.

There are no mistakes—only lessons. Growth is a process of trial and error and experimentation. You can learn as much from failure as you can from success.

A lesson is repeated until it is learned. A lesson will be presented to you in various forms until you have learned it. When you have learned it (as evidenced by a change in your attitude and behavior), then you can go on to the next lesson.

Learning lessons does not end. There is no stage of life that does not contain some lessons. As long as you live, there will be something more to learn.

"There" is no better than "here." When your "there" has become a "here," you will obtain another "there" that will again look better than your "here." Don't be fooled by believing that the unattainable is better than what you have.

Others are merely mirrors of you. You cannot love or hate something about another person unless it reflects something you love or hate about yourself. When tempted to criticize others, ask yourself why you feel so strongly.

What you make of your life is up to you. You have all the tools and resources you need. Remember that through desire, goal-setting, and unflagging effort you can have anything you want. Persistence is the key to success.

The answers lie within you. The solutions to all of life's problems lie within your grasp. All you need to do is ask, look, listen, and trust.

You will forget all of this. Unless you consistently stay focused on the goals you have set for yourself, everything you've just read won't mean a thing.

THE ROAD DOES NOT BELONG TO YOU ALONE

As you will learn in Road Rule #2, you must learn to **share the road** of life with others. This means that you must commit to anticipating the movements of others and to communicating your intentions to allow for mutual safe passage. You juggle visibility, time, space and thought all at once and hope that others are all doing the same. You will be respectful of not just the other cars on the road of life, but also the different <u>types</u> of vehicles which all come in many shapes and sizes and may include pedestrians, motorcyclists, bicyclists, animals, emerging vehicles and highway construction crews. All are on the road trying to reach their destination in their own way and at their own pace. You must know and respect the rules of the road – <u>ignorance or piety is no excuse</u>. You must anticipate those that will not follow the rules – <u>expect the unexpected</u>. You must know where you are going and how you are going to get there – <u>planning your navigational path will get you safely to your destination</u>. You must embrace the concept of kinetic energy to avoid the sin of complacency or you will not evolve forward – **inertia is the enemy of progress.**

THE 12 ESSENTIAL RULES FOR NAVIGATING THE ROAD OF LIFE

Chapter 1

Be The Truck.
Not The Squirrel.

"The highways are littered with the carcasses of people with
misguided or uninspired careers, underperforming engines,
blurred visions, dysfunctional drivers, and empty fuel
tanks, people who have been run over by stronger, faster,
and better moving vehicles along the road to success."
--Andrew J. Sherman

Each one of us has had that moment when we are stuck, frozen in time and without momentum, like a deer in headlights about to be struck by a truck traveling seventy miles per hour down the highway. In that life or death situation, we are either going to choose to get out of the way or to remain lifeless and dumbfounded by the peril. These eat or be eaten moments affect people at many different stages of their lives, their concerns, and their relationships.

THE ECOSYSTEM OF THE HIGHWAY

Think about the ecosystem of a typical highway. The most powerful vehicle is clearly the eighteen-wheel truck, its awesome strength and size confidently carrying valuable cargo to its destination. On the other end of the spectrum is the squirrel, whose indecision leads to its demise.

Trucks are strong, durable, versatile, and build on their momentum as they move towards their destination according to a road map and on a designated timetable. Nothing stands in their way as they slowly and steadily get to where they are going with confidence and purpose. On the road of life, have you put a game plan in place that will make you a truck? Or are you more likely to be the squirrel scampering from place to place with no clear destination? *Road Rules®* will allow you to gather the knowledge, insights, and wisdom you will need to truly be the truck and not the squirrel. By following these rules, you position yourself to harness the power of the truck and avoid the fate of the squirrel.

Squirrels are generally happy to eat acorns and mind their own business until one day they are in the wrong place at the wrong time. WHAM! They never knew what hit them. They are overpowered or blindsided by a force much greater than they are and their fate is sealed.

In today's unpredictable world and economy, it's more important than ever to position yourself to be the truck. Whether it is in your business or personal life, you have to remain focused or you will fritter away time, your most valuable resource, on small, near-term priorities, like finding the next acorn.

So how do you live your life like the truck and not the squirrel?

Here are eight critical aspects:

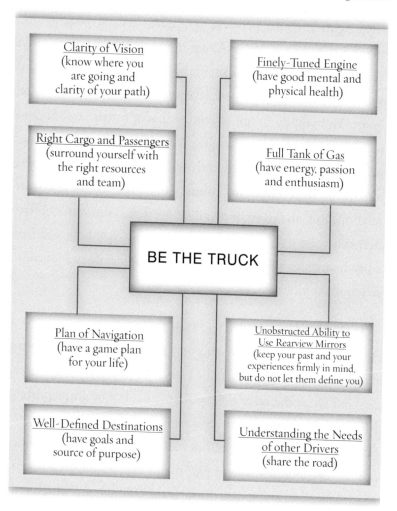

Being the truck does *not* mean barreling down the road forward without regard to what's in front of you or reaching your destination at any cost. The message of this book is that you should embrace and enjoy the ride towards your destination, always carrying a full cargo of knowledge ready to deliver and share with others. These are the rules to live by on the road of life. You are issued a driver's license as a privilege, not as a legal right, and that privilege is conditioned on your following the rules of the road. Along the path to your destination are many of life's lessons, some simple and straightforward and some that will require a few layers of the onion to be peeled away. Your ability to understand and adopt these lessons, and to truly apply them in defining your life's path and your actions, decisions and choices, etc, will all define your success as a person. Your ability to "connect the dots," to harvest your relationships and your intangible assets to ensure alignment between your core values and your actions, will help you live a productive, enlightened, and enriched life. Life is a journey, so enjoy the ride!

SOME PERSPECTIVES ON SQUIRRELS

Although there are some who consider squirrels to be essentially rats with long furry tails, I have no problem with squirrels, nor is the theme of this book intended to be anti-squirrel. I hope to avoid any nasty calls or e-mails from PETA or the SPCA as the result of the subtitle. After all, squirrels have some positive attributes: for example, the foresight and the knowledge to store acorns to last through the cold winter, which is a great life lesson.

The Simmons Society was founded by Professor Roger M. Knutson of Luther College in Decorah, Iowa, to further studies of road fauna...also known as roadkill. Professor Knutson has published a book called *Common Animals of Roads, Streets and Highways: A Field Guide to Flattened Fauna*. It probably does not lend itself to coffee table chats, but does contain some disheartening data. A publication called the *Animal People Newsletter* estimates that the following animals are killed by motor vehicles in the United States on an annual basis:

- 41 million squirrels
- 26 million cats
- 22 million rats
- 19 million opossums
- 15 million raccoons
- 6 million dogs
- 350,000 deer

If this data is correct, vehicles on U.S. roads are killing over 100 million animals per year, with squirrels occupying the unenviable position of being number one on the list. Many of the animals that meet their fate as roadkill share some of the same characteristics.

- They did not see their demise coming.
- They were killed by something much bigger and stronger than them.
- They reacted to a threat with inertia.
- They lacked the ability to escape their circumstances.

None of us should act in this fashion, yet too often we live our lives no differently than animals soon to be roadkill. We suffer from DITH Syndrome™ —Deer In The Headlights Syndrome. We either do not see danger coming or we see it, freeze in shock, and essentially accept our peril.

Who has the best perspective on the road? The squirrel sits two inches above the ground and can barely see much ahead of him. He lives in the present, with no perspective on the future or the past. Surely the truck driver who sits fifteen feet above the road has vision which is further and wider than everyone else. Where do you sit? How can you get a better view and clearer perspective on the road of life? What is your perspective on your life, your future, your family, or the hurdles that lie ahead of you and your goals?

Living a life dedicated to proactivity means that when life's challenges come at you hard and fast, do not stand there in shock, but rather develop the speed, attitude, training, skills, and ability to take action—or at the very least, get out of the way to avoid an accident. It also means having a game plan for reaching your destination, not wandering through life, which increases your chances of being a squirrel. The old saying that "if you don't know where you are going, then any road will get you there" provides some insight into the importance of defining goals as a precursor to actions.

YOUR PATH RELATIVE TO OTHERS THAT CAME BEFORE YOU

You are not alone on your path. Many others have walked it before you and many others will walk it after you. You will not be the only truck on the highway. The Earth is 4.5 billion years old and has just over 6.5 billion inhabitants. Every problem, every experience, every challenge you face has been faced before and should be examined on a relative basis. We have electronic access to technology that gives us a direct path to the knowledge, insights and wisdom of those who walked before us and have opportunities to share navigational tips for those who will follow in their footsteps. We have metaphysical access to the collective and limitless bounds of the human spirit and to the collective knowledge of all those who have lived before us. We have social access to the folklore, stories, and literature that teaches us how to navigate the new roads that lie ahead of us. It has been said that the only thing truly new in this life is the history we haven't yet learned or discovered. I am not sure that I accept this notion entirely on its face, but it does serve as a gentle reminder and source of comfort next time you face a problem or challenge that appears to be unique or insurmountable.

TRUCK DRIVERS AND LEADERS

From a core value and skill set perspective, many of the attributes that you would seek in an effective leader are the same that you would want in a truck driver:

- ⊙ Charts a clear path towards his or her destination

- ⊙ Stays focused for long periods of time without rest

- ⊙ Takes responsibility for valuable cargo

- ⊙ Understands that even the slightest mistake can cause significant harm to others

- ⊙ Knows the importance of navigating alternative paths in the face of logjams

- ⊙ Controls and harnesses the power and capability of his or her vehicle to stay within the boundary of applicable laws and norms

- ⊙ Uses skills and experiences to prevent the vehicle from crashing during a steep decline, and uses momentum and patience to climb steep upward hills

- ⊙ Communicates effectively with others

THE EIGHT CYLINDER ENGINE
FOR LIFE'S JOURNEY

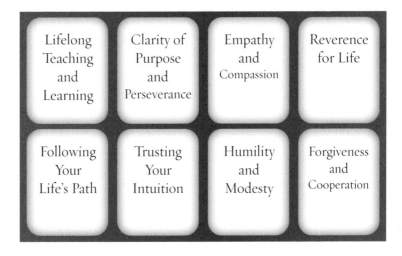

BEING THE TRUCK

To truly be the metaphorical truck that lies at the heart of this book, you must embrace and believe in the notion that you are in control of your own destiny. Your skill sets, your choices, your network, your street smarts, and your overall determination will greatly influence your outcomes and the consequences of your decisions. You are in control.

KNOW YOUR INNER DRIVER

It is my hope that some of the insights shared in *Road Rules®* will help you get to your true destination in life. But *how* you get there depends on you. We all have different styles, different approaches, and different ways of mapping out our journeys. We all have different sources of comfort and tolerance for risk. In many ways, our driving styles are reflective of our approach to the pace at which we intend to reach our destination. **Be in touch with your inner driver**. Understand how your driving skills behind the wheel may be in alignment with your driving style on the road of life.

CONSIDER THE FOLLOWING DRIVING STYLES:

- ⊙ <u>Hyper-Aggressive</u>—This driver is going to get to her destination as fast as she can without regard to others around her, the rules of the road, or common courtesies. Her chances of an accident are high.

- ⊙ <u>Man on a Mission</u>—This driver is strategic and methodical. He knows when to speed up and when to slow down, when to pass and when a speed trap may lie ahead.

⊙ <u>The Safari Adventurer</u>—This driver views every trip behind the wheel as an adventure. Side roads become her main roads. She embraces the journey, albeit sometimes too much. There is never a fruit stand that isn't worth stopping for or an antique shop that does not warrant "just a few minutes of shopping."

⊙ <u>The Plodder</u>—This driver moves at one pace: moderate. He takes moderate risks in life and reaps moderate rewards. He is not in a terrible hurry to reach his destination, but is deliberate in his actions. He is pleased with the pace of his life, even if not all destinations are reached quite as quickly as others.

⊙ <u>Slow Boat to China</u>—This driver puts safety first ahead of all other priorities, irrespective of its impact on her ability to reach her destination; she will drive forty-eight in a fifty-five speed limit zone. The irony is that in her attempt to avoid an accident she is actually endangering others by not keeping pace.

⊙ <u>Too Distracted to Focus</u>—This driver will never reach his destination because he is too distracted to focus. There is always a radio dial to adjust, a cell phone to answer, a text message to send; driving (and safety) are secondary to the many other tasks he seeks to accomplish while driving.

⊙ The Backseat Driver—This driver (who actually is not driving at all) takes more pleasure in directing others to do what she will not do for herself. Her ability to reach her destination depends on the actions of others, but she would like to dictate the course, the pace, and the methodology.

Which best describes you? Are you a different type of driver depending on the circumstances and road conditions? Do you have the ability to adjust your skills accordingly? Are you the driver you want to be? How do others perceive you? How is your driving style impacting the clarity of your view or the certainty of the path that you are on?

Each Jewish New Year, Rosh Hashanah, Jewish people all over the world consider the following self-reflection:

Who shall be truly alive and who shall merely exist;

Who shall be happy and who shall be miserable;

Who shall attain fulfillment in his days
And who shall not attain fulfillment in his days;

Who shall be tormented by the fire of ambition
And who shall be overcome by the waters of failure;

Who shall be pierced by the sharp sword of envy
And who shall be torn by the wild beast of resentment;

Who shall hunger for companionship
And who shall thirst for approval;

Who shall be shattered by the earthquake of social change
And who shall be plagued by the pressures of conformity;

Who shall be strangled by insecurity
And who shall be stoned into submission;

Who shall be content with his lot
And who shall wander in search of satisfaction;

Who shall be serene and who shall be distraught;

Who shall be at ease and who shall be afflicted with anxiety;

Who shall be poor in his own eyes
And who shall be rich in tranquility;

Who shall be brought low with futility
And who shall be exalted through achievement?

You have the free will to choose the answers to these questions and define your path. But to do so, you must commit to a life of proactivity—a life with both hands on the wheel, clear vision, a full tank of fuel, and a well-mapped route to reach your destination. You must also develop empathy and compassion for those that may never reach their destination and offer support and encouragement for those who will pass you by. We must all be guided by the brutal reality that nothing lasts forever except the legacy that you leave behind. How do you want to be remembered by the other passengers and drivers in your travels?

Life. Strap on your seatbelt, take a deep breath, and get ready for a wild and bumpy ride.

Chapter 2

Share the Road

Sow a thought and reap an act
Sow an act and reap a habit
Sow a habit and reap a character
Sow a character and reap a destiny.
                              —*Thich Thein-An*

In one of many famous *Seinfeld* episodes, Jerry complained to George that he allowed another driver to cut in front of him but the other driver failed to give him the "courtesy wave" as a thank you. Jerry facilitated the othe driver's passage in an act of kindness and just wanted a simple thank you as part of the expected "culture of the road." The show made an important point: Our society has lost sight of the importance of basic courtesies in our communities and in the marketplace. Yet many of us miss them. Multiple statistics have shown that most workers would forfeit significant financial raises and bonuses in exchange for even increases in recognition, trust, and mutual respect. Research also shows that customers will gladly pay higher prices if treated with appreciation, professionalism, and a smile.

We all must learn to share the road of life with each other. This means that each of us must commit to anticipating the movements of others and to communicating your intentions to allow for mutual safe passage. You juggle visibility, time, space and thought all at once and hope that others are all doing the same. You will be respectful of not just the other cars on the road of life, but also the different types of vehicles which all come in many shapes and sizes and may include pedestrians, motorcyclists, bicyclists, animals, emerging vehicles and highway construction crews. All are on the road trying to reach their destination in their own way and at their own pace. As we learn in driving school, a commitment to being the truck is not just about you. It also means being considerate of the needs and destinations of all the other drivers and being aware of all of the other vehicles on the road. It means understanding the navigation and staying on the right path can be difficult and requires skills, focus and patience. When you see on the back of every 18-wheeler the following words: "Caution: This Vehicle Makes Wide Turns," it should serve as a reminder of the fact that teamwork, communication, patience and experience are the critical conditions needed to avoid collisions.

Close your eyes and take a minute to think about your travels on a typical highway. We are all traveling at speeds of seventy miles per hour, inches away from one another. We are betting our lives on the assumption that the drivers on either side of us will respect the painted lives that separate us and are paying enough attention to the task at hand to avoid swerving into our lane and bring both of our journeys to an abrupt and painful ending. We hope and pray that each driver is not tired, inconsiderate, distracted or under the influence of drugs or alcohol in a fashion which will diminish the quality of their concentration or ability to stay within their lane.

Why is a commitment to **sharing** the roads on which we pursue journeys so critical? Why do we need to understand and respect the written laws and unwritten road courtesies in order to ensure that we all arrive at our intended destinations in a safe and enjoyable manner? Why must we avoid aggressive driving or tailgating—which by definition means that we are following someone so closely that neither of us have enough space to change lanes or adjust our paths without collision? Why can't we acknowledge the fairness of tollbooths, when we must stop for a minute and pay a small price for maintaining the cost of a road? Where are the toll booths in your life? Did you slow down and make your contribution? Or did you try to speed through it without paying to avoid a two-dollar toll only to wind up with a two-hundred-dollar ticket? And did you have a kind word for the toll both operators, who suffers through one of the most boring jobs on the planet on a daily basis?

Gandhi said, "Be the change that you wish to see in the world." We must all focus on being better drivers on the highway of life, not just talking about how bad the other drivers are, how irritating traffic has become, or how torn up our roads are. In a world following the events of September 11, 2001, and the corporate failures and scandals of Enron, Worldcom, Tyco, and Adelphia, all of us want to work for a company built on principles of accountability and that understands basic decency and common courtesy and be part of a community that respects and embraces its neighbors. Being the truck and not the squirrel means that you understand and adopt integrity as one of your core values and always give a "courtesy wave" when a fellow driver yields the road to you unexpectedly and unaggressively, even if they don't see it or acknowledge it. It has been said that integrity is what you do and the decisions you make when nobody is looking. Integrity and a commitment to others cannot be driven by a desire for praise or recognition by them. First it must be motivated by an inner sense of peace and core values. Trucks understand that building character and acts of kindness and simple recognition—a smile, a gesture, a pat on the back, or a high five—can all go a long way. Squirrels forget to take basic human nature into account when traveling their path and, in the process of elbowing one another aside to get ahead, are the first to get hit by the truck.

We taught our two children at an early age to never forget to say "please and thank you," and as a result, they rarely forget to do so. What we insist on early, reinforce often, and lead by example *can* and *will* happen. If you insist on integrity, character, and a commitment to core values, and then reinforce and reward their importance, walking the talk by acting consistently with your beliefs, you'll be pleasantly surprised by the level of goodness that will come back to you tenfold and show up in the conduct of your children and grandchildren. You never know when your car will breakdown on the side of the road or when you'll unexpectedly drive into a ditch. At that moment in time, you'll need help. Someone will need to take themselves off their path to help you get back on your own. What goes around comes around. The more you are willing to help others who are stranded on the road of life, the more help you will get when the favor needs to be returned. It is always better to be in the act of making large deposits to the "chit" bank than to be overdrawn. You truly get what you give on the road of life (and then some).

ROAD RAGE IN THE MODERN AGE

I do not think it is all in my imagination that driving conditions are getting worse not better. On a typical commute to work, I am cut off three to five times; the other drivers appear to not even know that I am there—or really care. We are in a bigger hurry to get wherever we are going than ever before. There are more of us and less adequate roads. There are more cars and less good drivers. There is more frustration and less common courtesy. We are more distracted and far less focused—or so hyper-focused that we disregard the needs of others. We seem to increasingly believe that <u>our</u> need to arrive at our destination is far more important than everyone else's need to do the same.

Reported incidents of violence traced to road rage have increased significantly over the past few years, and all it takes is forty-five minutes on a crowded highway to know that the problem is not going away any time soon on its own. We talk on cell phones, send text messages, eat breakfast, flip through two hundred channels of satellite radio, put on makeup, shave, etc. It's amazing that we still have time to actually drive.

Our inability to deal with each other properly on the roads is starting to spillover to the highway of life. There was a brief moment of time after the incidents of September 11,

2001, when we seemed to care more about each other collectively than ourselves, but that seems to have evaporated in favor of a society riddled by stress, a lack of time, and an impatience to reach our misguided destinations. We lead lives filled with contrast, irony and insincerity. On my way to work recently, an eco-friendly hybrid car with a bumper sticker that read "Practice random kindness and senseless acts of beauty" was weaving through the traffic at a frenzied pace, barely avoiding a series of near collisions. These inconsistencies between our purported beliefs and our actions are the root of most of the stress in our society. We want to embrace and do the right things but our actual conduct sends a message otherwise to our fellow drivers. The tide needs to start turning in the other direction or we are heading for the mother of all traffic jams.

Just to clarify, I am not suggesting that any of us will enjoy a stress-free ride on the road of life. Stress in limited quantities helps fuel our passions to complete a given task and can make us more productive. My good friend and client Dr. Robert Rosen recently wrote a book called *Just Enough Anxiety* which teaches leaders and organizations how to create the right balance between anxiety and complacency in growing companies. The issue is not whether we will experience stress along the road of life, but rather what we do with it and how well we can manage stress to avoid an accident. We all could benefit by easing up our grip on the wheel just a bit and reconnecting with the joy and passion connected with the act of driving.

COURTESY TO PASSENGERS

In the song "Thunder Road," Bruce Springsteen sings, "The door's open, but the ride ain't free." He implies that you can join me in my vehicle, but you will live by my rules. In the late 1990s, Volkswagen ran a series of television advertisements that revolved around the theme "Drivers Wanted," implying that *passengers* on the road of life were less important. How many times have you told one of your own passengers, "Hey, it's *my* car, we listen to *my* music!" or "I'm driving, I make the rules." Sharing the road also means sharing it with passengers in your vehicle—especially on the road of life, where your "passengers" include your spouse, your children, your neighbors, your friends and co-workers. Your conduct as a driver affects all of your passengers, both on the road and in life. Each of us has been a passenger at some point, and in taking on this role we entrust our lives and our welfare into the hands of the driver—the ultimate act of trust and transfer of control.

Being respectful of your passengers and understanding that they are along for the ride with you—voluntarily or not—must guide your actions, your decisions, and the consequences of your choices. Is it okay to drive too fast or recklessly when your passengers have asked you to slow down or drive more carefully? Ask any driver who experienced a fatal collision in which they survived but one or more of their passengers did not.

Why, in our society today, are so many people neglecting their passengers? My suspicion is that we've become so laser-focused on financial rewards that there's almost no positive reinforcement for someone who, for instance, forestalls career success temporarily because a family member, whether a young child or an aging parent, needs them. There's relentless pressure in the workplace to put work first. And in our society, we seem to value work-related success above any other kind.

MANY DIFFERENT TYPES OF CARS ON THE ROAD

There are many different types of cars on the road, each with a right to reach its destination and travel its path with dignity, respect, and opportunity, regardless of whether it is blue or green, expensive or inexpensive. We must embrace and appreciate the diversity of the many vehicles that we will encounter on the road of life. Hmm, sound like any other life lesson?

We all talk about a commitment to embracing diversity—but what does that really mean? We must be careful not to preach the virtues of diversity and then place boundaries around how to define it. I can assure you that if we define *diversity* with words like *tolerance* or even *inclusion*, our society is truly doomed. Nothing good ever came out of the statement, "I tolerate you." Those are not words likely to foster cooperation or collaboration. And "inclusion" sounds too much like what your mother told you to do as a child when referring to a tagalong younger sibling. Again, not a word likely to inspire you to greatness. To include is not necessarily to embrace, and to tolerate is not necessarily to appreciate.

We must learn to embrace others if we are to truly appreciate each other and respect each other's paths (and maybe even help each other get there along the way). We must *want* to learn more about the backgrounds of others and what they can contribute to our own lives. That genuineness of emotion cannot be mandatory or dictated; it must be voluntary and self-motivated. Diversity can be harnessed into a powerful tool for creativity and innovation, but only if each member of the group respects the differences of each individual and embraces the perspectives they bring to the table.

To truly recognize the rights of all cars on the road of life, we need more carrots and less sticks. We must treat each other with respect and appreciation not because some law tells us to, but because we *want* to do so. We also cannot be over-anxious to "check the box" and move on to the next societal problem—like the environment or healthcare—just because we were nice to somebody different than ourselves during an isolated incident. Our genuine interest must be a lifetime commitment. Being kind enough to once let another driver into the lane ahead of you will not solve the problem of our nation's crowded highways, but if we all do it because we want to and know that it will be done for us when we need it, imagine how much more smoothly traffic will flow.

THE DICHOTOMY OF FEAR AND GREED

Why share the road? Well, why do anything in life? Why get out of bed in the morning? Why go to work? It is often said that our two primary motivators in life are *fear* and *greed*. It is true that many of our actions in life can be traced back to either our desire to get something that we want or out of fear of the consequences of our actions if we do something wrong or fail to take action when we knew that we should. To act out of fear may inspire the action, but it does not often yield the best results or the desired outcomes. Fear of the unknown tends to paralyze us. Fear of failure can impede our growth, creativity, innovation, invention, and advancement. And a fear of the consequences that may come from failure will only make us dread it even more and block our ability to either learn from the process of failing and our inhibit willingness to get up, brush ourselves off and try again. We would still be living in caves and driving vehicles that resemble the Fred Flintstone-mobile if we allowed our fears to truly be our only motivators. Same goes for greed. Being motivated by greed alone will lure you into the belief that all roads, all lanes, and all pathways to a desired location belong to you and you alone. You begin embracing the belief that there is only one room at the hotel at the top of the mountain that you intend to climb, when in fact there are many. You begin believing that there is only one path to your destination, when in fact there are many. You begin believing that you must win at the expense of others at any cost, when in fact there is plenty of road for all of us to share. Yes, the rungs do get harder and harder as we climb up the ladder, but you are not unique in your ability to climb the ladder—nor should you feel free to step on the hands and feet of others along the way.

Why can't we redefine the paradigm? Why can't we embrace a new set of "*Road Rules*"® in which our true motivators include education as both teacher and student, a passion for helping others, love, family and relationships, or a quest for knowledge or non-material things? Can we not all become enlightened drivers that enjoy the ride even more than arriving at our destination?

DON'T LEAVE YOUR CAR IN A NO-PARK ZONE

A key aspect of sharing the road is also only to park in designated areas. Parking your vehicle in a no-parking zone or double parking on a busy street only impedes the flow of traffic and slows everyone else down due to your selfish acts. What makes your path, your errand, or your priorities so important that you have the right to restrict the path of others? We seem to have lost sight of the anticipated and unexpected consequences of our actions. You were too busy over the weekend with your errands to fill your tank with gas and are now stalled out on a busy Monday morning, blocking a critical lane on an already congested highway into the city. The "domino" effect of your selfishness is now causing thousands of others who share this road with you on a daily basis to be late for work, an interview, a doctor's appointment, a critical meeting, etc. just because you had to have those shoes on sales at the mall two towns over on Sunday. Whether you meant to affect others in this fashion or not, the consequences of your decisions and priorities could have been anticipated and therefore avoided.

As you pause from the road of life to rest your vehicles in a parking lot or metered space, be cognizant of not overstaying your welcome. Tennessee Williams once said, "Sometimes there is a need for departure, even when there's no certain place to go." There will be situations in your life in which it is just plain old time to move on, even if it remains unclear where you are going next.

PLAYING TOUR GUIDE

Our information age and connectivity has created a new paradigm for knowledge and wisdom in the twenty-first century. We gain wisdom by tapping into a greater source of a shared pool of information. The Wikipedia® phenomenon has driven us all to share more, do more together, and collaborate and communicate in different fashions and through different media than five, ten, or twenty years ago. We watch each other's "home movies" on sites like YouTube®, learn more about each other's interests on sites like MySpace®, Friendster® and Facebook®, and buy each other's old stuff at prices we establish on eBay®. We meet each other in different ways, make collective decisions in different ways, and govern ourselves in a more connected fashion than we could have ever imagined even a decade ago.

We live in a world where *we* trumps *me* and where none of us alone are smarter than all of us together. We have all become tour guides in those areas of knowledge that we possess. Yet our frustrations upon arriving at a crowded parking lot or a bumper-to-bumper highway have not passed. All of those "other" cars force us to park hundreds of yards away from the entrance to the mall or to move too slowly on the freeway, and so we want them to disappear. Instead, why can't we rejoice and relish in the wisdom of these crowds? Why can't we smile at the fact that so many other people have chosen to be at the same place as you at the same time? How wise we must all be! How good those shops must all be!

Clearly, we judge other experiences in this fashion. A restaurant with a two-hour wait, or a sold out movie , or a stadium jam-packed with screaming fans, or a hotel with no available rooms become that much more attractive as we embrace and accept the notion that if so many others are going to that place, well then, it must be pretty good! We can't have our cake and eat it, too; life doesn't work that way. We cannot embrace crowds when it is convenient and let them frustrate us when it's not. As one small business owner told me, "I always hated big groups of people until they started showing up in my store."

As you travel the road of life, you accumulate knowledge and experiences that really have no value until they are shared with others—sometimes for a fee, sometimes for free. You decide. Zagat's® is a famous company that writes up restaurant reviews and then sells them to you on a city by city basis. Craigslist® and many other online sites form their lists of favorites, likes, and dislikes, and publishes and shares this information at no cost to the end user. I am less interested in the business model you choose (at least until I write *Road Rules® for Entrepreneurs!*) as I am with this important lesson—**once you arrive at your destination, it is your responsibility to play tour guide to those heading in your direction.**

It is the responsibility of all of us to give back once we have arrived—to share resources, knowledge, wisdom, insights, navigational advice, and encouragement to those on their way to the destination at which we have already arrived, to the roads we have already traveled. There has always been a place in every society for the shaman, the medicine man, the mahatma, the healer, the teacher, the guide, the prophet, the elder statesman, the sorcerer, the wizard, the mentor, the coach, the guru, the master, whose primary role in a community is to play "tour guide" for the benefit of others and the benefit of the overall good. This is the only way that we advance as a society, the only way true collective wisdom and wealth are created. It is your honor and duty to share your stories with others in order to appreciate the lessons learned during your journey (and its detours) and the significance of the place at which you have arrived. As you pause to inhale and absorb the beauty of the mountain vista, the wisdom of those who have climbed even higher mountains awaits, whenever and if ever you are ready. But in the interim, take your job of tour guide very seriously. There will always be someone trying to figure out how to get where you are, and always someone who has already been where you want to go.

We all have opportunities to be teachers, mentors, coaches, advisors, guides and sounding boards. There is always someone who will need and appreciate a few words of advice or guidance – whether in the context of the family, the workplace, the athletic field or the community center. Be proactive in your quest to fill this gap without intruding or offending others or offering your opinion or insights to people or in circumstances where it is not needed or warranted. When I began teaching over twenty years ago, it was initially to augment the lost income when my wife chose to focus on the raising of our two children. But economic benefits were quickly replaced with psychic rewards and it gives me immense professional satisfaction to know that thousands of students have in some way gained by the sharing of my experiences and the insights of my many guest lecturers. To this day, I get a chill down my spine when I get an e-mail or phone call update from a former student who relates to me some success that they have had in their lives as a result of taking one of my courses. *You don't always need to be the driver to share in the satisfaction of others reaching their destinations.*

GRAB A PICK AND A SHOVEL

In addition to your obligation to help others as a tour guide, we must all be responsible for highway maintenance. The efforts needed to keep the road of life in good condition cannot be fully delegated to road crews and state agencies. Our responsibilities as drivers are to fix something when we see it is broken, to avoid littering and to stop to help another driver in distress. We share these responsibilities as a society in order to ensure access and mobility on the highways that we travel together. Our journey should also include a commitment to the environment that surrounds our roads, including steps to reduce pollution, increase recycling and conserve the use of costly fuels. These roads of life that we all travel will only remain passable if we all contribute to their upkeep on a collective basis.

SPEED TRAPS AND THE FUZZ

Sharing the road also means following the rules of the road—respecting the rules of operation of your vehicle for the safety of yourself, your passengers, and everyone around you. The consequences of violating those rules can range from fines and penalties, loss of driving privileges, incarceration, injury, and even death. State troopers and local law enforcement agencies are in place to enforce these rules and to respond to accidents. But they cannot be everywhere at the same time. We must follow these rules because we want to and because they make sense to us, not because we fear a ticket or an accident. The same principles apply to life. When we respect the rights of others or go out of our way to help one another, it cannot and should not be motivated by the risk of a penalty. There will always be limitations on the upside of the things you do because you "hafta" but limitless possibilities to the things you do because you "wanna."

Speed traps are a fascinating phenomenon. The police hide in places out of view with sophisticated technology to catch us barreling down the road too fast. We buy radar detectors (where legal) to get advance warning and slow down before being trapped. This highway "guerilla warfare" is all in place to ensure that we are doing the things that we are all already supposed to do for our own safety and for that of those around us. And now more states and municipalities are installing speed cameras to further monitor driver conduct.

Where are the speed traps and cameras in your own life? Who are the "policemen" in your world who help keep your lives in order? What penalties and punishments do you fear as a motivator for your actions or inactions? And should these fears of repercussion be the proper tools to guide your actions or decisions?

BEEPING YOUR HORN TOO LOUDLY OR TOO OFTEN

Those who beep their horns nonstop while driving just get ignored and are irritating and distracting to other drivers. Beeping your horn correlates to when and how you should raise your voice. Those who yell at anyone at anytime and in any situation live their lives with the Boy Who Cried Wolf syndrome; they are never taken seriously. Choose your battles carefully and only show emotion when it is a truly hypercritical situation. Although this general rule of thumb is a credible life lesson, it is interesting to note international cultural differences. When driving in the crowded streets of India where drivers are often only centimeters apart, a gentle tap on the horn is an accepted form of communication, asserting, "I am right here, just in case you don't notice me." This custom avoids many accidents but is kept to a quick and gentle tap of the horn to ensure clear communication.

SHARE THE ROAD

You do not need to take up all of the lanes to get to your destination. And when you do make an error, you do not get to correct it by putting others in peril. How many times have you seen another driver pull dangerously onto or off the highway, cutting across lanes without regard to others? *You do not*

have the license to endanger others trying to get to their destinations just because you have misjudged your own. Share the road with others ... there are generally enough lanes to go around. You only get one lane per customer. Take what the defense gives you. Work with what you have; not all lanes will be available to you at all times.

Driving too slow on the highway of life can be just as dangerous to those around you as driving to fast. We have ranges of expectations as to pace and speed on each road that we travel and rely on each other to stay within those optimal ranges when on those roads together for each of our safety and serenity.

In the powerful film, *Into the Wild*, a recent college graduate travels alone deep into the wilderness to discover the true meaning of life. As he lies dying hundreds of miles away from civilization and having left behind many people who care deeply for him, he etches into a piece of wood the only true life lesson he learned in his quest:

"HAPPINESS IS ONLY REAL WHEN SHARED."

No man is an island. We are not put on this earth to be alone, nor are we here to only benefit ourselves. The roads we are on, the paths that we walk, and the highways that we travel are *meant to be shared*. The happiness comes from reaching our destination while sharing the road with others, without rage or collision.

CHAPTER 3

HAPPINESS IS A CLEAR WINDSHIELD

"In the land of the blind, the man with one eye is king."
—Ancient Chinese proverb

I was born with a congenital cataract, leaving me blind since birth in my left eye. I do not have the same peripheral vision or depth perception that people with vision in both eyes do. When I was a youth, doctors told me to focus on sports with bigger balls, such as basketball and football. Unwilling to accept this life sentence of limitations, I sought out the sport with the smallest ball that I could find—squash—and by age twelve had won a local tournament in Philadelphia.

Many years later, the irony of my life is that while I do not physically see as well as 99.5 percent of the population, I am paid as a legal and strategic advisor to see the things that nobody else can see. In building companies and organizations, leaders and founders are typically too close to the forest to see the trees. Outside advisors are brought in to help them have clearer vision of their growth path, to bring clarity to their mission, to share best practices and experiences, to help them understand the big picture, and to help them realize what business they are *really* in.

I recently spent the day with a company that had been in business for twenty-three years but did not understand what business they were really in and what assets they had available to harvest. Yet I saw their strengths within an hour. Perhaps they were blinded by the light of opportunity or by the darkness of frustration. My malfunctioning eyes have served as the guide for hundreds of companies, from early-stage to rapid growth to middle market, Fortune 500, and even Dow 30 companies. Clarity of vision does not require a set of eyes that perform on a 20/20 basis.

It has been said that teaching others means to help make the invisible visible. To help others see what can't be seen— at first—is to help them develop the tools to see beyond their current horizon or break through the barriers that are clouding or restricting their vision. It is no coincidence that when we speak of those who are on a path of lifelong learning, we refer to them as *enlightened*.

It amazes me just how blind we all can really be and how foggy we allow our windshields to become. It really comes down to how you define yourself and your perspective and attitudes towards your own limitations. I have never viewed myself as being "half blind" but only as someone with impaired vision who will need to work a little harder than others to see everything that needs to be seen. What impairments to vision have you had to overcome? In what ways have you allowed these impairments to become real impediments to your goals or successes? In what ways would a redefinition of these actual or perceived impairments change your perceptions of your own limitations? If you allow your perceptions of your weaknesses define you, then they most certainly will—and in doing so, you are giving others tacit permission to define you in the same manner.

We are surrounded by examples of people who have overcome challenges and burdens far greater than our own. Lance Armstrong overcame cancer to win multiple Tour de France races. Magic Johnson dealt with the challenges of HIV and became a very successful entrepreneur. This kind of heroism transcends the celebrities you read about in *People* magazine. There are attitudinal heroes that live in your neighborhood, whose names you may never know; but their acts, commitment, and perseverance serve as a model for us all. There's the emergency room physician who comes home every night to spend time with her child with severe autism. There's the postman who delivers your mail every day whose uniform covers the multiple wounds that he suffered in Vietnam.

In fact, a recent study by the Cass Business School in London suggests that certain types of impairments and disabilities can actually *enhance* success in business or career path. For example, 35 percent of the entrepreneurs who were studied suffered from dyslexia; many others had mild to severe forms of ADD or ADHD. The individuals studied were forced at an early age in life to develop compensatory skills to overcome these challenges. **In other words, they had to become extra strong in certain areas to offset weaknesses beyond their control.** Many in the study learned the importance of mentors, of delegating to others, of trust, teamwork, and other traits to adapt to their weaknesses, which turned out to be strengths in business and grit and determination as an adult. They are in good company—business leaders with dyslexia include Richard Branson, Charles Schwab, and John Chambers. Challenges in an ability to read was transformed into razor sharp intuition and a willingness to delegate critical tasks to others.

We all have our burdens, restrictions, and afflictions to overcome. This is not a "woe is me" message about "misery loving company" but rather a wake-up call to never allow *what* you are to define *who* you are. Never allow your history to dictate your future. Never allow your physical impediments to be a barrier to your levels of accomplishment. Never allow the false perceptions of others to cloud your vision, goals, and dreams.

<u>Sources of Inspiration</u>

Next time you're feeling sorry for yourself or stuck in the rut of believing that whatever your real or perceived disability to progress may be, get in your car and go to your favorite video rental store and check-out any or all of these films which remind us how critical it is to look beyond our challenges:

- ⊙ "My Left Foot"

- ⊙ "Blindsight"

- ⊙ "Ray"

- ⊙ "The Miracle Worker"

- ⊙ "The Mighty"

- ⊙ "The Other Side of the Mountain"

- ⊙ "Ruby"

- ⊙ "The Terry Fox Show"

THE BLINDSPOTS IN OUR LIVES

Every car has a blindspot, some more than others. Where are the blindspots in your life? Where are things happening that may affect your fate but you can't see them and therefore can't anticipate their consequences? How many times do we feel like "Man, I did not see that one coming!" and are relieved when there is no collision? In our cars, blind spots can often be minimized with mirror extenders as well as training ourselves as drivers to know where the blindspots are for a given vehicle and adjusting our driving accordingly. What steps can you take to mitigate the blindspots in your life? Where could you add windows and mirrors to enhance the quality of your vision?

"A HARD RAIN'S GONNA FALL"

One of the most prolific songwriters of our time, Bob Dylan, warns us in the heading above that storms can come down pretty hard to cloud our vision—though he offers solace in another of his songs, *Shelter from the Storm*. And yet another great band from the 1970s, Creedence Clearwater Revival, offers us hope in *I Can See Clearly Now, the Rain Is Gone*.

No matter where you live, rain will fall and cloud your vision. A crystal clear path to your destination is an illusion. It is a misnomer to think that you will be able to avoid the fog, the rain, the snow, the ice, the stalled engines, the flat tires and the general fatigue that life will challenge you with from time to time. So what adjustments will you need to make to restore clarity? Bob Marley reminds us in one of his great lyrics, "When the rain come down, it don't fall on just one man's house. Just remember dat." When I first learned to drive, wiper switch speeds came in two speeds, fast or slow—but life was simpler then. Today's owner's manuals teach us that we have many alternatives: there is the mist wiper setting, multiple choices within the intermittent setting, the low speed operation, and the high speed operation. On a concurrent path, I am adjusting temperatures and fan speeds on my defoggers, defrosters, and de-icers. Wow, that's a lot of work to maintain clarity of vision—but it sure beats running into a tree or another driver. It's not just rain that can impede your vision; those sun visors are there to help ensure that you are not "Blinded by the Light" as Manfred Mann or Bruce Springsteen would say.

Recognize that you'll never have *all* of the clarity that you would like to have at any given moment. The Swiss philosopher Henri Amiel once wrote, "The man who insists upon seeing with perfect clearness before he decides will never decide anything."

AVOIDING COMPLACENCY AND THE IMPEDIMENTS TO CLEAR SIGHT

Growing up in Philadelphia, living in Baltimore, and raising a family in the suburbs of Washington, D.C., has blessed me with the joy of all four seasons and therefore all possible sets of driving conditions. In thirty-two years of driving, one of my many "pet peeves" is when other drivers do not completely clean their cars following a snowstorm, leaving themselves only with a frontal "peephole," and then get on the road with snow, sleet, and ice ahead of them. These drivers have significantly increased their chances of endangering themselves and others by failing to properly clean their cars, not to mention those wonderful moments when the residual snow and ice that they have left on their vehicles comes flying at you at sixty-five mph because they have chosen to let gravity do their chores for them. ***These drivers allow complacency to cloud their vision to the point of harming others.*** The extra ten minutes that it would take to enjoy the benefits of a clean windshield (as well as side mirrors and rear window) are within their grasp, but selfishness or laziness get in the way. The same rules apply to removal of dirt or bird droppings, morning dew, pollen, and film, or to fog, smoke, haze, or anything else that stands in the way of clear vision.

If you need to refill your metaphorical windshield wiper fluid, replace worn down wiper blades, or get your defogger to work properly, then be proactive and make it happen. If you have the power to remove impediments to your vision, do so without delay. Never, ever be complacent or reactive in accepting a clouded outlook when you have the ability to enjoy clear sight. Just ask anyone who is vision-impaired what they would do to change their condition, and you will appreciate my strong feelings on this Road Rule.

Our ability to thrive, perform, succeed and enjoy life relies on our ability to see things clearly, to make the right decisions and to have all of the information and perspectives available to us to make these decisions. If we have the power to remove the impediments to our vision, we should do so with gumption and without delay.

ZEN AND THE ART OF TRUCK DRIVING

"The Master in the art of living

makes little distinction between

his work and his play,

his labor and his leisure,

his mind and his body,

his education and his recreation,

his love and his religion.

He hardly knows which is which.

He simply pursues his vision of

excellence

in whatever he does,

leaving others to decide

whether he is working or play.

To him his is always doing both."

—Zen Buddhist text

It is often said, "do something that you love and you'll never work another day in your life." Finding your true purpose is critical to an enlightened and enjoyable existence as well as to maintain and enhance clear vision on the road of life. Strength and inner peace comes from knowing that we are doing with our lives what we were intended to do and contributing to society in ways that fully harvest our strengths. Everyone should ask themselves, "Is the job that I am doing and the tasks that I am performing my 'highest and best use' to the organization, to society, and to myself?" Most successful people I know do not separate the concepts of work and play. To them, all of their actions meld together as being part of their life's purpose.

One common mistake made by people in determining whether they are on the right life or career path is the selection of a job or profession because they are good at it rather than choosing the things that truly make them happy. This tends to cloud vision and delays arrival at the intended destination. It is human nature to assume that because we are good at something it must be what we should be doing. But *good* and *should* are not the same. Fulfillment in life will not come from the material things or money but are more likely to come from understanding what makes us the happiest. The challenge is whether we can achieve Zen master status by finding a way to align the good and the should, so that there is ultimately no distinction between the two.

When was the last time you experienced true joy, intense emotional excitement, <u>or</u> a fiery passion while doing the things you call work? Do you have the faith to put yourself on a path where those emotions can be an every day occurrence? What hurdles stand in your way? Are they concrete barriers, or just speed bumps? I would urge you to examine these perceived barriers more closely.

WHICH PERSPECTIVE?

Are you too focused on looking in your rearview mirror when you should be spending more time looking out your front windshield? Or vice versa? Some of us are so caught up living in the past that we cannot lean forward to envision the future.

Others are too quick to look ahead, failing to learn from their past. Good drivers are focused on their futures without losing sight of their pasts. We learn from our history … but it cannot define us. We embrace our history...to appreciate our progress. As my father-in-law, Max Joffe, used to say, "Don't forget to look in your rearview mirror often enough to remind you as to how far you have travelled."

DEFINING YOUR LIFE'S PATH

> *"What lies behind us and what lies before us are*
> *small matters compared with what lies within us"*
> —*Ralph Waldo Emerson*

Emerson could not be more on point. Each of us owes it to ourselves, to our families, to our friends, to our co-workers, and to our society to not go to the grave with our song still in our hearts. We owe it to ourselves and to each other to walk the path that we are intended to travel. Our inner peace, our energy, our passion and commitment are all harvested from the comfort of knowing that we are doing with our lives what is intended for us and that there is alignment between our true talents and chosen occupation and related activities. Only then can we experience the benefits of a truly clear windshield.

Take a minute to write down some answers to the following questions:

⊙ What activities make me the happiest?

⊙ What are my inner strengths?

⊙ What am I as good at as anyone I know?

⊙ In what ways do my own opinions of my strengths compare to how others perceive them to be?

⊙ Is there an alignment between perceptions and reality?

Consider your answers carefully. Then take just a few more minutes to answer the following questions:

⊙ What is my game plan for life and my personal mission statement?

⊙ How will I define my personal brand, values, and core beliefs?

⊙ How will my legacy be defined?

⊙ What impact will I make on this world?

⊙ What are the things most likely to be said about me at my funeral? How will what is said compare to the true feelings of people who remember me?

⊙ What might my epitaph and/or obituary say? Do they read the way I want them to? What will I do to change them now while I still have the chance?

There is a great story about Alfred Nobel, who had devoted his professional life to the study of explosives and was the inventor of dynamite. When a French newspaper in 1888 prematurely published his obituary and condemned him for his contributions to the world, it occurred to him that his legacy would always be as a person who pioneered a means of mass destruction. Hoping to change his legacy before it was too late, he endowed a series of five Nobel peace prizes, which are now some of the world's most recognized honors.

Over the past twenty-five years, I have realized that my true path in life is as an educator. Finding your true purpose in life is very liberating and provides amazing clarity, though things do not always manifest themselves exactly as you envision or in manners which are traditional. For example, my calling in life as the "blue collar scholar" (as one who is devoted to education notwithstanding my relatively unimpressive academic pedigree and upbringing) takes on many forms throughout a typical week – as a transactional and corporate lawyer, as an author, as a partner of a prominent law firm, as a public speaker, as a board member, as an MBA professor, as a husband, as a father and as a friend. Not all forms of teaching yield the same level of economic rewards and not all students will learn the same way or be as receptive to the wisdom that you want to share.

Living your life as an educator also means devoting yourself to lifelong learning. You must always keep your mind open to absorb, process and then share the benefits of your experiences and insights. A true teacher has the power to inspire others – a light that cannot kindle other lights is but a feeble flame.

Becoming a true teacher, however, is a process, not an event, as aptly-put by <u>Kahlil Gibran</u>:

> *"In seeking knowledge and enlightenment,*
> *the first step is silence,*
> *the second listening,*

the third remembering,

the fourth practicing,

and the fifth – teaching others."

It means dedicating yourself to the belief that there is only one good, which is knowledge, and one evil, which is ignorance. A true master teacher is not the one with the most students, but the one who has created the most masters. Being a lifelong teacher also means understanding how to adjust your style, your message and your methodology to reach someone who is resisting what you are teaching. We all learn things in different ways and your job as the instructor is to adapt your delivery accordingly. It also means to stay calm and patient when your students are slow to learn ….or refuse to listen. It is difficult to teach those whose minds and hearts are not open to improvement, to help those who do not want to be helped or to offer a solution to someone who won't admit they have a problem.

DON'T FEAR THE REAPER

"People will forget what you did, people will forget what you said, but people will never forget how you made them feel."
—*Maya Angelou*

I do not fear death. I fear not being remembered. I fear living an incomplete life. I fear the possibility of not helping all who need assistance or not teaching all those who want to learn. I fear not loving enough. I fear not living enough. We are all on this earth to make a positive impact and contribution to the greater good. An impact on one another, an impact on science or technology, an impact on our community, our government, our society, our planet. ***An impact, not a collision.*** The impact of the events of 9/11, the sniper shootings, the events at Columbine and other schools, malls, and on public transportation—all within the past ten years—have been a horrible reminder of a simple truth: none of us know which day will be our last. That does not mean that we should take the phrase "Live each day is if it were your last" to the extreme, or we would all quit our jobs and go pursue whatever is the number one thing on our "goals in life" list. But I would recommend that we take a slightly modified approach on a *daily* basis to ensure that we have minimal regrets on our deathbeds. Give some thought to the things you have always wanted to accomplish, the places you have always wanted to go, and then "chip away" at the list on a more modest and incremental basis.

Remember, this is more than putting checkmarks next to items on a lifelong to-do list. Ask yourself how you want to be remembered. How have you made people feel? In what ways have you enhanced or improved the lives of others, be they family, friends, co-workers, or neighbors? When is the last time you attended the funeral of someone that you knew pretty well? What was said about that person? Was that how you knew them? Is that how you will remember them? Do you wish you had taken the time to get to know them better while they were still alive?

Harriet Beecher Stowe once wrote, "The bitterest tears shed over graves are for the words left unsaid and the deeds left undone." When we keep our best thoughts to ourselves and our best acts inside of us, it constipates our existence, serving as a road block of insurmountable proportions to the reaching of our destinations. In the film, *The Bucket List*, Morgan Freeman explains to Jack Nicholson that in certain cultures, only two questions are asked as conditions to admission to the pearly gates of heaven: Did you find joy in your life? Did you bring joy to others?

CHAPTER 4

EMBRACE YOUR DASHBOARD

When is the last time that you really, really looked at your car's dashboard? When did you take the time to appreciate all of the information it can teach you about your car … and your life?

What if our bodies came with gauges, indicators, and warning lights? What if we could analyze the performance of our lives and the paths we have traveled, what if we understood the exact speed and level of effort it took for us to reach our destinations? What if we could extend our lives and improve our health by paying more careful attention to our indicators and warning lights? Well, we can!

In growing a company, a common adage is that you will **manage what you measure**. In other words, the key business indicators and ratios that are paid the most attention to are likely to be the areas that are likely to strengthen and improve. A successful CEO will build a dashboard populated by the gauges and indicators that monitors daily, weekly, monthly, and quarterly. He will manage effectively by **inspecting what he is expecting** from his team. He will ensure that there is proper communication of the behaviors that he wants from his employees by reinforcing and connecting rewards to the actions that will empower the company to reach its goals.

As CEO of your own life, the same principles apply. To be the truck and not the squirrel, you must customize a dashboard around your own dreams, goals, and aspirations. This will only be effective if you pay careful attention to the data that is provided to you and adjust accordingly. It is also important to pay attention to the dashboards of other drivers around you. It is often said that the sum of a person's life is to measure yourself by the people who measured themselves by you.

WARNING LIGHTS

The National Highway Traffic Safety Administration estimates that twenty million people per day continue to drive their vehicles even when a key warning light is on—often for days, weeks, or even months until they have time to bring their car in for service. We are all guilty of doing the same thing with our lives. We often ignore key warning signals that our minds, bodies, or intuitions are trying to send to us until the damage has already been done to our health, our relationships, our families, or our careers. A warning light is clearly visible, yet we choose to ignore it or postpone dealing with it until it is too late.

BUILDING YOUR DASHBOARD

Take the time to build your own dashboard based on your life plan, your goals, your interests, and your commitments to improve or change your life's current conditions. Carefully monitor your progress in these areas and pay attention to the flashing red or yellow lights that may be warning you that it is metaphorically time to refuel, change or recharge your battery, add some necessary lubricant to gears and pistons that are underperforming, or replace spark plugs that are dull and lifeless. Just like your car, your dashboard for life will be populated with these six types of measurement guides:

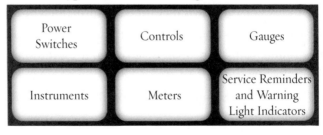

Power Switches	Controls	Gauges
Instruments	Meters	Service Reminders and Warning Light Indicators

BUILDING YOUR DASHBOARD FOR LIFE

How can you mimic the functions of your vehicle's dashboard to give you a better handle on how you are doing in life and whether you are on track to reach your destination?

ODOMETER
How much life is left in my vehicle?
What roads have I traveled?

TACHOMETER
How hard is my engine working to get more efficient productivity?

SPEEDOMETER
How fast am I going?

TRIP METER
How far have I you traveled on this particular journey?
What did I learn?

POWER SWITCHES
What buttons do I need to press to make things happen?
Where can I learn how and when to press the buttons?

EMERGENCY FLASHERS
When should I reach out for help?
What signals can I use to warn others that hazardous conditions lie ahead?

GAUGES

Do I have enough fuel to reach my destination?

Am I running low on fluids?

Is my engine overheating?

WARNING LIGHTS AND BUZZERS

Do I pay careful attention to these warnings and get things fixed or do I delay and ignore cautionary sight?

Have I fastened my seat belt and am I ready for the ride?

How much juice is left in my battery?

TOW LIMIT WARNINGS

How much weight can I haul?

How much can I carry for another without putting my own vehicle in jeopardy?

ENGINE WARNING LIGHTS

When should I take myself in for immediate service, maintenance, or repair?

SEAT HEATERS

Oh, wouldn't that be nice to have for life, but it would destroy the coat, sweater, and sweatshirt industry!

COMPASS AND OUTDOOR TEMPERATURE

In what direction are you moving and what weather conditions might you encounter?

CUSTOM DASHBOARDS AND NEW GAUGES

There are certain gauges and meters that ought to be on everyone's life dashboards, even if they do not relate to driving a car. You can build your own custom dashboard based on your goals, priorities and challenges, but here are a few of my own:

EXPERIENCE O'METER

There is a big difference between knowing the path and walking it. Geography is the art of learning where things are, but archaeology is the science of digging deep into the inner core and touching the earth and its relics. You learn to sift through what is valuable and important vs. what is just old junk. There are too many armchair philosophers running this world that have developed strong opinions on matters that they have never actually experienced. This meter measures the difference between thoughts and experiences.

WHINING LIGHTS

An ironic situation that would have upset most people came up for me at work recently. When confronted by the head of our department, I responded, "No worries, I am laughing louder than I am crying." Many recent studies have demonstrated that laughter, smiling, and general happiness and lack of stress can extend your life, and reduce the chances of heart disease and even certain types of cancer. Those with poor outlooks, high negative stress, constant whining, and bouts of self-pity are more prone to depression, suicide, and a generally less gratifying time on the planet. Our whining light warning light should go off when we really need to adjust our perspective or when way too much time has passed between a radiant smile or a deep belly laugh.

PRIORITY O'METER

Things that matter the most must never be at the mercy of the things that matter the least. All of us—myself included—could do a much better job establishing our priorities and managing our time around what is truly important in life. Our time is our most valuable asset and yet usually our most wasted resource. How can we allow ourselves to be careful with our money and so cavalier with our time? It is the one thing you always want more of as you near death, and the one thing you can never get back once it is lost.

Time Flying Out The Window | Time Management Aligned With Priorities

PASSION GAUGE

Cadillac ran an advertising campaign for its STS vehicle in 2007 with the theme "When you turn your car on, does it return the favor?" If you accept the basic premise of *Road Rules®* that driving is a metaphor for life, then how excited are you when you get behind the wheel every day? Have you stayed connected with the thrill of driving? Or are you just passing through? Find the passion, the energy, and the enthusiasm that you need to make even the simplest of drives to the food store an adventure, a journey, and an opportunity for learning. It is all about perspective. Last week, it took over ninety minutes in traffic to reach Redskins Stadium from my home—a trip that should have taken thirty. I had the choice of allowing the horrible traffic to ruin my evening or view it as an additional sixty minutes with my eighteen-year-old son who was soon to leave for college. I chose the latter.

INSTRUMENTS OF FATE AND FAITH

One of my favorite stories is about a man who dies and confronts God at the gates of heaven. He says to the Lord, "I was a good man. I went to church every Sunday, observed the Ten Commandments and gave my children a strong sense of their heritage. I prayed and prayed, and all I asked was that once, just once, you would have allowed me to win the lottery. It never happened and now here I am." To which God replies, "It would have really helped if you had bought a ticket."

We cannot drive our cars on the road of life guided only by blind faith. We cannot expect our religious beliefs—whatever they may be—to help us if we do not help ourselves. This dashboard gauge would remind us to step things up when we are falling into the trap of relying too heavily on others to get us to where we want to go and where we need to be.

CLARITY O'METER

Consider the following—another great story from religious roots that provides some insights:

> Two traveling angels stopped to spend the night in the home of a wealthy family. The family was rude and refused to let the angels stay in the mansion's guest room. Instead they were given a space in the cold basement. As they made their bed on the hard floor, the older angel saw a hole in the wall and repaired it. When the younger angel asked why, the older angel replied, "Things aren't always what they seem."

The next night the pair came to rest at the house of a very poor but very hospitable farmer and his wife. After sharing what little food they had, the couple let the angels sleep in their bed where they could have a good night's rest. When the sun came up the next morning, the angels found the farmer and his wife in tears. Their only cow, whose milk had been their sole income, lay dead in the field. The younger angel was infuriated and asked the older angel, "How could you have let this happen? The first man had everything, yet you helped him. The second family had little but was willing to share everything, and you let their cow die."

"Things aren't always what they seem," the older angel replied. "When we stayed in the basement of the mansion, I noticed there was gold stored in that hole in the wall. Since the owner was so obsessed with greed and unwilling to share his good fortune, I sealed the wall so he wouldn't find it. Then last night as we slept in the farmer's bed, the angel of death came for his wife. I gave him the cow instead. Things aren't always what they seem."

We need a meter on our life dashboards that prevents us from making a lazy or surface-level interpretation of a series of events or expected consequences. Our analytical skills have become soft, and we fail to dig deeper into a situation to understand its true meaning. We must have the discipline to gather facts and consider as many perspectives as we can *before* arriving at a decision or cause of action. Our challenge is that we are now a society that values speed—we want our answers fast and furious in headline fashion and at the speed of light. We are quick to come to conclusions without all of the facts. We make incomplete decisions and hasty remarks. We make our plans around a set of facts that are "an inch deep and a mile wide." The Clarity O'Meter is our reminder of our quest for truth, informed decision-making, avoiding premature judgment, and reading the entire story, not just the headlines.

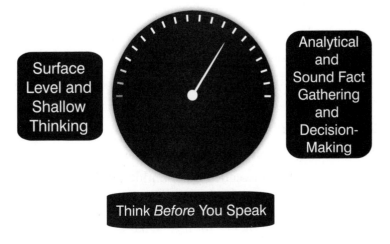

NET CONTRIBUTION GAUGE

For all of us to advance as a society, we each must be committed to giving more than we get, to contributing more than we extract, and to adding more than we subtract. We need to measure from time to time what we are giving to this world vs. what we are taking from it. Otherwise, the deficit will surely destroy us. Commit to bring to the table *more* than what is obvious or expected, even if it takes a little more effort.

THE ELEGANCE OF ONSTAR®

The rollout of OnStar® by General Motors a few years ago was a stroke of financial and marketing genius. Not only did it create a real and valuable competitive edge for car buyers and consumers that offered tangible value in the areas of emergency assistance, directions, and concierge services, but satisfied the "priceless" piece of mind that so many drivers are willing to pay for in today's turbulent times. The financial stroke of genius was to leverage an income stream on a monthly basis from the car buyer which transcended the monthly car payment or the interim maintenance revenues.

Identify your OnStar® for life. What is your contingency or emergency plan? Who can you count on 24/7 to help you in a time of need, no matter what, at the press of a button? Would you do the same for them? Those little blue and red buttons that sit on our lives' dashboards may not be the ones we use the most often, but we are comforted by knowing that they are always there.

WEIGHING THE METRICS

As you begin to use your life dashboard more effectively, try to develop a weighted system for ranking and prioritizing the things that are most important to you and which determine your happiness and drive you towards your destination. Much of our life is spent gathering the relevant variables that influence our analysis, ranking them and then making an informed decision. The most typical metrics may be the number of dollars sitting in your bank account or the encouraging lab results after your annual physical check-up but there's more to life than cash and cholesterol. What other metrics can you monitor? What other variables influence whether you are satisfied or you are frustrated? The weather? The results from last night's game played by your favorite sports team? The performance of the stock market? I would urge you to consider some new metrics to help guide your relative daily happiness, such as: the health and welfare of your family and friends, the satisfaction of your work and respect of your peers, your contributions to the community, etc. Imagine being in a bad mood at the end of the day because you felt you did not help enough people or hug your kids enough times instead of whether you had to navigate through a bad traffic jam or the Dow Jones® index dropping by 100 points!

CHAPTER 5
PAY CAREFUL ATTENTION TO THE ROAD SIGNS OF LIFE

And the sign said,

"Long-haired freaky people

Need not apply."

So I tucked my hair up under my hat

And I went in to ask him why.

He said, "You look like a fine upstandin' young man.

I think you'll do."

So I took off my hat and said, "Imagine that.

huh, me workin' for you."

Whoa, sign, sign.

Everywhere a sign.

Blockin' out the scen'ry.

Breakin' my mind.

Do this. Don't do that.

Can't you read the sign?

And the sign said,

"Anybody caught trespassin'

Will be shot on sight."

So I jumped on the fence and I yelled at the house,

"Hey! What gives you the right

To put up a fence to keep me out,

But to keep Mother Nature in?
If God was here, he'd tell you to your face,
'Man, you're some kind of sinner.'"

Sign, sign.
Everywhere a sign.
Blockin' out the scenery.
Breakin' my mind.
Do this. Don't do that.
Can't you read the sign?

Now, hey you, mister, can't you read?
You got to have a shirt and tie to get a seat.
You can't even watch. No, you can't eat.
You ain't supposed to be here.
The sign said, "You've got to have a membership card to get inside."

And the sign said, "Everybody welcome.
Come in. Kneel down and pray."
But when they passed around the plate at the end of it all,
I didn't have a penny to pay
So I got me a pen and a paper
And I made up my own little sign.
It said, "Thank you, Lord, for thinkin' 'bout me.
I'm alive and doin' fine."

Whoo! Sign, sign.

Everywhere a sign.

Blockin' out the scenery.

Breakin' my mind.

Do this. Don't do that.

Can't you read the sign?

Sign, sign.

Everywhere a sign.

Sign, sign.

— Signs *by Five Man Electrical Band*

F or many of us, the signs along the road are perceived like the lyrics of the song above – filled with distractions, detours and contradictions to the pace and to the manner in which we want to travel. But what if these same signs also had hidden lessons for us and could also be guideposts for our journey on the road of life? How many road signs do we pass each day that have messages that transcend well beyond their literal meaning? Here's an easy one:

SLOW: Children At Play

When you see this sign driving, slowly is obviously the right thing to do. But it is also a reminder of an important life lesson. Take your foot off the accelerator long enough to spend time with your children and with your family. It is a reminder of the regrets that so many of us feel when we blink our eyes and suddenly are "empty nesters" suffering from woulda/coulda/shoulda syndrome, wishing that we had slowed down enough to spend more time with our children when they were younger. How many of us speed through our children's lives or go too fast through opportunities for education and learning because we are too focused on the end result?

ROAD SIGNS = LIFE SIGNS

Most road signs have basic insights to guide you along the highway of life. Speed limits, stop, yield, steep declines or windy road warnings, one-way streets, no thru street, dead end, etc., offer life lessons for us. But we are driving past them too quickly to notice or are so focused on getting to our destinations that we don't take time to read them or think about the wisdom that they share.

STOP VS. YIELD

Some intersections in life require a full stop, an examination of the situation before moving forward. Others are more of a yield. They remind you to slow down a bit and take notice of what is around you before you proceed at full speed, but it's usually okay to glide through with caution. When in your life have you slowed to a complete stop when you should have kept your momentum? When have you kept going when you should have stopped completely and contemplated your situation? When would it have been advantageous to have observed what was ahead before launching right in?

Here are some additional *Road Rules* to consider next time you see some of the road's most common signs:

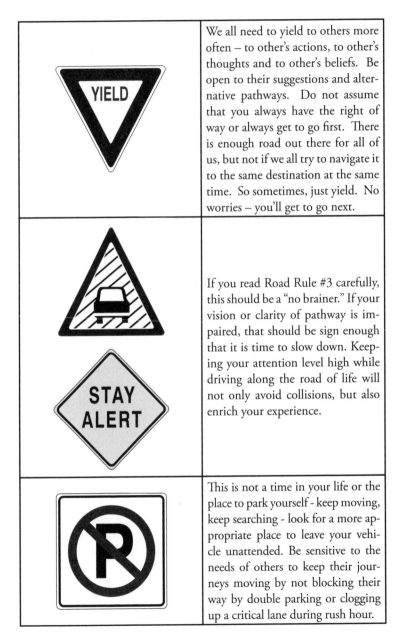

YIELD	We all need to yield to others more often – to other's actions, to other's thoughts and to other's beliefs. Be open to their suggestions and alternative pathways. Do not assume that you always have the right of way or always get to go first. There is enough road out there for all of us, but not if we all try to navigate it to the same destination at the same time. So sometimes, just yield. No worries – you'll get to go next.
STAY ALERT	If you read Road Rule #3 carefully, this should be a "no brainer." If your vision or clarity of pathway is impaired, that should be sign enough that it is time to slow down. Keeping your attention level high while driving along the road of life will not only avoid collisions, but also enrich your experience.
(No Parking)	This is not a time in your life or the place to park yourself - keep moving, keep searching - look for a more appropriate place to leave your vehicle unattended. Be sensitive to the needs of others to keep their journeys moving by not blocking their way by double parking or clogging up a critical lane during rush hour.

 **SLOWER TRAFFIC KEEP RIGHT**	If you want to travel at a slow or moderate pace in life, that is your prerogative; but do not get in the way of others who want to move a bit faster. By traveling in the wrong lane, you are merely in their way and creating expectations about your own pace of travel that are not consistent with your actions.
DO NOT ENTER	Wow—I wish that I could have paid more attention to this sign when I was dating back in college! How many relationships should we have never started or places we should have never gone? If only a sign could have warned us not to go there in the first place! How many career paths or job opportunities should we have avoided? How can we fine-tune our navigational skills to avoid traveling certain paths?
 **CAUTION MEN WORKING**	Don't speed past and endanger people working in teams when they are trying to be productive. If you cannot add something to the process, do not interfere, impede, or endanger it. Be respectful to those that are trying to make your pathway more passable
 **DEAD END** **NOT A THRU STREET**	Both of these signs should require little explanation. Some of the paths that we travel will be fruitless; there will be no pot of gold at the end of the rainbow and we need to turn around and begin anew. Learn how to recognize them and move on.

NO EXIT	Very Sartre-like—we can enter but we can't leave, a bit like the accommodations in the lyrics of the Eagles' "Hotel California." It's probably best to know the details of the check-out policies (or lack thereof) well before checking in.
EMERGENCY STOPPING ONLY	You are truly on the right path in life! Keep going and charge forward at maximum allowable speed. Do not swerve from your current path unless or until you sense danger or an emergency.
	If you are carrying heavy or dangerous cargo, it's probably best to let someone take a look at it once in awhile to make sure that you are following the rules of the road and not carrying too big of a load, which could slow you down or endanger you or others. Be careful not to over extend your commitments on a personal or professional front – our eyes of desire are visually wider than the capacity of our stomachs of commitment.
LANE ENDS MERGE LEFT	Pay careful attention to changes in your roadway of life that are truly inevitable. You may be cruising along in your lane of choice, only to learn that you will be out of runway sooner than you expected.

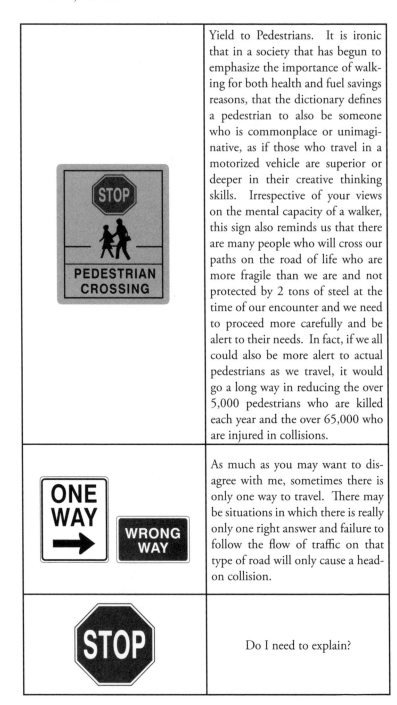

	Yield to Pedestrians. It is ironic that in a society that has begun to emphasize the importance of walking for both health and fuel savings reasons, that the dictionary defines a pedestrian to also be someone who is commonplace or unimaginative, as if those who travel in a motorized vehicle are superior or deeper in their creative thinking skills. Irrespective of your views on the mental capacity of a walker, this sign also reminds us that there are many people who will cross our paths on the road of life who are more fragile than we are and not protected by 2 tons of steel at the time of our encounter and we need to proceed more carefully and be alert to their needs. In fact, if we all could also be more alert to actual pedestrians as we travel, it would go a long way in reducing the over 5,000 pedestrians who are killed each year and the over 65,000 who are injured in collisions.
	As much as you may want to disagree with me, sometimes there is only one way to travel. There may be situations in which there is really only one right answer and failure to follow the flow of traffic on that type of road will only cause a head-on collision.
	Do I need to explain?

PRIVATE ROAD **NO THRU TRAFFIC**	Yes, this is America, land of the free, but it is also the land of the rights of the property owner. Trespass is the ultimate form of disrespect for these property rights, but does not seem to stop us from driving or parking on the roads or in the spots that only a few taxpayers have underwritten. Give respect to get respect.
NO **VEHICLES BEYOND THIS POINT** **NO** **TRUCKS ALLOWED** **NO** **BICYCLES** **PEDESTRIANS PROHIBITED**	Here's a news flash—some roads are really only meant for cars and some are too narrow to allow for trucks. The lesson is that not all means of transportation are meant to travel on all roads in life. Know the difference and adjust your navigational route accordingly.
SPEED BUMP AHEAD	My all-time favorite statement of the obvious. Speed bumps are designed to be a subtle or not-so-subtle reminder that you are now driving on road conditions or in neighborhoods where you need to slow down and proceed with caution. The fact that we need a sign to warn us of the presence of an upcoming speed bump that is designed to force us to slow down has always been very ironic to me.

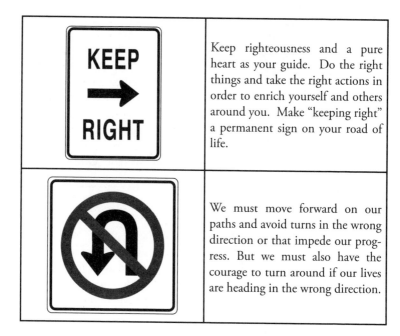

KEEP → RIGHT	Keep righteousness and a pure heart as your guide. Do the right things and take the right actions in order to enrich yourself and others around you. Make "keeping right" a permanent sign on your road of life.
	We must move forward on our paths and avoid turns in the wrong direction or that impede our progress. But we must also have the courage to turn around if our lives are heading in the wrong direction.

BILLBOARDS AND NON-TRAFFIC SIGNS

Up until this point in the chapter, our focus has been of the life lessons we can garner from federal, state, or local signs placed by the highway to guide us in our driving by an authority. But that is not the only "eye candy" we experience on our journey. There are countless billboards and advertisements that communicate with us and influence our behavior. Some are very innocent, like "Scenic View 1000 feet ahead[1]" while others are a bit more ominous, such as "BEST BURGER IN THE

---

1 By the way, when is the last time you pulled off the road for five minutes and actually stopped to take in the scenic view? Your tax dollars paid for a ramp and a rest stop so that you could enjoy the beauty of Mother Nature—but you probably just drive right by! Take some time to smell the roses.

WORLD—NEXT RIGHT." If you don't stop, you are left wondering if you just passed by the culinary experience of a lifetime at sixty-five mph. There are many non-traffic signs and bright and shiny billboards in life seeking to influence our decisions or allocate our purchasing power. Some want us to spend money, others to cast a vote, others to establish goodwill and brand recognition, others to watch a particular television show and a few just to get us thinking about life.

Gone are the days when billboards were limited to thirty-foot tall signs above the highway or messages painted onto a public bench. Today's world of outdoor advertising has become very sophisticated. The Outdoor Advertising Association of America (yes, there *is* a trade association for everything in the United States) boasts more than 1,100 members which enjoy over eight billion dollars in sales, from traditional billboards to outdoor signs to transmit advertising and street furniture to "alternative outdoor" that includes signs in public bathrooms, on beaches, mobile phones, airplane seat tables, lamp signs, on the bottoms of swimming pools, on escalator steps, in elevators, on outdoor sculptures, drains—if you can imagine it, there is a sign for it telling us what to do, what to think, or what to buy. We are truly surrounded by signs. Even religion has gotten into the act with the now world famous "messages from God" (my favorites are "Don't Make Me Come Down There," "Life Is Short. Eternity Isn't," "Keep Using My Name in Vain and I'll Make Rush Hour Longer," and "It's a Small World. I Know. I Made It.") to the hundreds of churches that have ten- and fifteen-word mini-sermons on their mantles.

WHAT'S YOUR SIGN?

Road Rule #5 teaches us that the more we can pay attention to the hidden messages and insights that the signs and billboards in our lives are trying to teach us, the smoother and more enjoyable will be our journey. As James Redfield emphasizes in *The Celestine Prophecy* we must develop a heightened awareness of the lessons being conveyed and suspend our doubts and distractions long enough to "connect the dots" and take a hearty gulp from the goblet of wisdom. Or we can pass by these signs at neck-breaking speeds, missing out on the guidance that they offer. But let's look at the consequences of disregarding signs, even at a literal level – you are likely to get lost, fined or cause an accident if you disregard many of the street or highway signs along our roads. But to ignore the highway signs of life can have even greater consequences, resulting in a potential loss of love, opportunity, understanding, peace, wisdom, health, comfort, or even life. Redfield's Fifth Insight reminds us that these signs can provide us with all of the wisdom we need for our journey but only when and if we open our minds to their teachings.

CHAPTER 6

BE GUIDED BY YOUR NAVIGATIONAL SYSTEM

"Failing to plan is planning to fail."
—*Unknown*

Everybody talks about the importance of having a life plan, and I could not agree more. I have seen too many squirrels head aimlessly into a dark tunnel with no light in sight because they were clueless about where they were heading or what it would take to find the other end. Trucks have to plan routes that take into account low underpasses, commuter traffic, limited lanes, and "cars only" highways. It is much more of a challenge for them to reach their final destination than regular cars, and it is impossible to do without careful planning. The trucks and their drivers understand the discipline of planning and enjoy the benefits of their actions.

Each of us must build a navigational system for our lives. A life plan must be articulated, not only to yourself, but to family members and others that will be affected by your vision – your life passengers – to make sure they are along for the ride and then it is our navigational system helps keep us on that path. And on this long journey, be prepared for the periodic (or not so periodic) question from your anxious passengers that we as parents have all heard: "Are we there yet? Are we there yet? When are we getting there and at which rest stop can we go to for ice cream?"

We all use different types of navigational systems while driving—some of us have the pre-installed systems in our cars, some add an electronic GPS system later, and some rely on memory, instinct, traditional maps, landmarks or even others in the car for guidance as to how to reach our destination. Some of us are even humble and brave enough to admit our mistakes and ask strangers for directions when we are lost, putting ego and pride aside in favor of the need to get to where we are going. Whatever your navigational tool of choice may be—or some combination thereof—it is critical that you take the time to build an effective navigational system to guide you on your life's path.

Navigational systems help us reach our destination in an efficient manner, but they can also serve other important purposes. Properly built, they can help us maneuver our way out of a metaphorical (or real) traffic jam, help us identify sources and locations of food, fuel, and lodging, and warn us of the dangers or delays that lie ahead. We can rely on a visual depiction or screen, or we can enable that subtle, even sexy but often annoying little voice that tells us to turn left in fifty feet, instructs us to veer right at the next yield, or chides us when we make the wrong turn. If only that little voice was also available in life situations. Imagine your navigational device sharing helpful hints like:

"Avoid this relationship."

"Leave this job."

"Run, don't walk away, from this salesman."

or simply

"You are not heading down the right life path."

Well, guess what? It is available. That little voice known as our *subconscious* speaks to us during 100 percent of our waking lives. Our instincts and gut feelings, *are* that little navigational device that is wired into our brains and our bodies. But how often do we listen to that voice, follow our instincts, or trust our gut feel? The answer should be almost always but for many of us it is almost never.

To be the truck and not the squirrel, you must commit to paying more careful attention to these life navigational aids that you have had since birth.

NAVIGATIONAL TOOLS

Whether you prefer an old fashioned map or have a car equipped with the latest computer navigational device, understand that these are tools, not a crutch. In a very memorable episode of the NBC sitcom *The Office,* the general manager, played by Steve Carell, drove his rental car directly into a lake, even though it was clearly in front of him. Rather than trust his instincts, he followed the verbal instructions of the navigation device. Don't ever let this happen to you in life or in business. Use the devices and tools available to get you to your destination, but **trust your gut** for the final decisions and to make adjustments to the route plan that may be necessary.

LIFE PLANNING AND NAVIGATION

It is often said, "If you don't know where you are going, then how can you ever know whether you get there?" Most of us get behind the wheel of our cars with a specific destination in mind, yet we are driving into the great abyss when it comes to defining our life's destination, our personal goals, and where we hope to be heading.

Look carefully at your answers to the questions articulated in Chapter 3. How can you adapt these answers into a life plan that will enrich you and your family with inner peace and financial and non-financial wealth? How much dust has collected on any plans you made for yourself five, ten, or even twenty years ago? Even if you have achieved your financial goals at this point, are you *truly* fulfilled? Have your health, happiness, and self-reflection goals been obtained? Even Winnie the Pooh knows the importance of a game plan; A. A. Milne writes, "Before beginning a hunt, it is wise to ask someone (or yourself) what it is you are truly looking for before you begin looking for it." Rarely does an "I'll know it when I see it" approach really work, especially if you have been traveling on the road of life at seventy mph.

For some of us, a lack of inertia is sufficient. We may be content with the feeling that we are moving forward in the right direction, even if we are not too sure where we are headed or are traveling at a slow pace. We live our lives with a partial blindfold on at all times, letting life happen to us instead of attempting to influence its direction. For others, mere survival is sufficient. I'll ask some of my friends what their aspirations may be or what their New Year's resolutions include, and I'll get answers like "staying above ground," "staying away from debt collectors," "avoiding my ex-wife," or "losing twenty pounds."

And while those are all admirable goals, they are short-term and small-minded in nature, and not a substitute for a life plan, a vision, and an articulation of true goals. **Avoiding death is an insufficient game plan for living life.** Once you take the time to articulate your life long goals, it will be a lot easier to then build a navigational system to guide you and ensure that you are on the right path making the right decisions. This will expedite the reaching of your destination with a minimal amount of bumps and bruises along the way.

Life planning is an imperfect art and a less than exact science. The fortune cookie message which reads "Man Plans and God Laughs" does have some wisdom. As I approach 50 years of life, there are many events that I could have never anticipated, but these contingencies have only enforced, not diluted, my belief in the need for a game plan – but it must be carefully monitored and adjusted often to be effective. Life does get in the way of the best laid plans, sometimes unexpectedly to the upside and all too often painfully to the downside. I have spent time with friends and colleagues who abruptly and horribly lost their spouses or even their children to cancer or a car accident and the process of recalibrating your life plans following such a tragedy is brutally challenging. As a late-stage baby boomer, many of us are at the age where we will be putting our parents to rest in the not too distant future. With their final trip to the exit ramp plainly in sight, have you adjusted your plans accordingly? Have you done what needs to be done? Have you said what needs to be said? Ask anyone who has been through these types of challenges and their responses will all be the same

– you cannot stop living, you cannot stop planning and you cannot stop dancing down the highway of your own life. As another great lyric in the Eagles song *Hotel California* observes: "Some dance to remember and some dance to forget."

Driving and life are all about planning and anticipation—planning your route and choosing your lanes based on your destination, thinking ahead, and anticipating the moves that will be made by others. Of course, we will all be caught by surprise from time to time, but do you really think that the driver of the car in the far left lane of a five-lane highway that suddenly realizes that her exit is coming up and cuts across four lanes without regard to anyone else has an effective life plan? Do you think that she somehow magically thinks about the impact of her actions on others? Your driving style is often a reflection and an insight as to how you live your life. How many people do you know whose driving styles relfect their lifestyles? The "go slow and I'll get there whenever I get there" guy may also be the same person whose career has not advanced in many years. The "I'll get there at any cost" guy does reach his destination faster, but increases the chances of a crash or burn-out or alienating a lot of people along the way. The "I will navigate my way creatively around this traffic guy" always has a strategy and a fallback plan. It is also important to realize that your bad driving habits are not as opaque or anonymous as you think they are.

Next time you consider an inappropriate gesture or aggressive driving manuever, either on the road for cars or the road of life, pay careful attention to your audience and those you are about to affect. What if it is your boss, your client, your neighbor? More than once in my life I have over-honked my horn nearing my office only to find that I have directed my frustration or aggression at a fellow co-worker, a fellow partner, and once even at a client who was on his way to see me!

I often wonder if we would all drive our cars – and our lives – differently if our most critical life passengers were with us at all times. Would you really tailgate the car in front of you and aggressively cut off other drivers if your children were in the back seat? Then why do so when they are not? Because guess what? If you collide with another car, the consequences to your family will be virtually the same as if they were actually in the car with you. Same goes for the road of life. As mentioned earlier in this book, character is defined by the conduct you choose and the decisions you make when nobody is looking and nobody is around. Would you make those same decisions if your parents, spouse or children were watching your every move? Your students? Your co-workers? Don't be fooled into believing that only your conduct in front of others is the measure from which you will be observed or judged by others. Drive on the road of life as if you have a club van filled with important lifelong passengers – because you do.

VISUALIZATION AND NAVIGATION

Many of us will visualize a route in our minds before embarking on our travels (or we should). We see the roadblocks, the hurdles, and the detours and then work around them. The same rules apply to our navigation of the road of life. Stephen

Covey and others have written extensively about the power of visualization. The second habit of Covey's *The 7 Habits of Highly Effective People* is "Begin with the End in Mind." Covey teaches us that through creative visualization, we can bring our dreams closer to a reality by looking at the future in the present moment in our minds. I strongly agree with this core concept as an effective tool for life or business planning (as well as safe and efficient driving).

THE BEAUTY OF TRAFFIC REPORTS

If you are anything like me, one of the first things you do after getting in your car is to turn on the radio for the latest traffic report. It is a thing of beauty, knowing in advance where the blockages and delays to my journey are so that I can navigate around them accordingly. Whether these delays are due to weather conditions, highway construction, fender benders, or just traditional congestion, an energetic voice over the airways warns me of the challenges that lie ahead and that helps me adjust my route and my schedule accordingly.

Nobody likes traffic jams. The time delays and general stress and frustration have caused me to miss flights, be late for important meetings, and say things to others drivers that I now regret--but living in a large East Coast city for all of my life, I have accepted them as inevitable. As such, I begin to plan around them by leaving earlier to reach my destination or attempting to maximize my productivity and enjoyment while stuck behind the wheel. We must learn to adapt and adjust to the unpleasant circumstances in our lives when we know they cannot be avoided and do our best to turn them from lemons into lemonade.

What if we could tune-in to a traffic update for our journeys along the road of life? What if a voice was available at any time that we turned on the radio to give us fair warning of the hurdles that lie ahead so that we could either adjust our timetables or seek an alternative route? There may not be too many reliable crystal-ball readers available, but we do have the ability to raise our awareness and sensitivity to signs that will help us forecast our futures. If you are not clear yet on this concept, go back and re-read Road Rule #5. These signs, signals, instincts, advice, and guidance are among the navigational tools available to you to determine whether an alternative route should be taken, as discussed in the upcoming Road Rule #7. The critical point, of course, is to take the time to listen to the "traffic reports" that are available to you before embarking to your destination and listen again at multiple points along the way.

Building your life plan is a marathon, not a sprint; it is a process, not an event if you draw a strategic parallel to a NASCAR® season (e.g. a series of long races as you accumulate experience, victories, and defeats towards a long-term goal), you will understand that you do not necessarily need to win every race to reach your goals or destination.

Have you drafted a life plan that will navigate your course, identifying the skills, talents, relationships and resources that you will need to get there? Does it assume that you will always win each battle or does it stay more focused on winning the war? Does the plan include a sensitivity analysis to anticipate the inevitable surprises that life will throw at you? Or the "what ifs"? If you have drafted a plan a while ago, then you may need to dust if off and look for the necessary adjustments and updates that can or should be made.

NAVIGATION BY NEGOTIATION

Our life's journey will involve many compromises. The boundaries of compromise are established through the art and science of negotiation. While a detailed treatment of negotiation is beyond the scope of this book, there are a few things worth sharing as part of the tools you'll need to navigate properly. Understand first that **negotiation is a process by which two parties come together to solve a problem, each with the desire to satisfy their own needs for mutual gain**. Data gathering on what really matters to the other person is what is critical it will yield far better results than manipulation or game playing. Having negotiated hundreds of transactions both large and small, I have found that the most successful negotiations are when the parties each feel that they got their cake but may be a little disappointed as to the flavor or amount of the icing (and not everyone can get the flower on top). The goal is to deliver the *core* that each party needs and hopefully "horse-trade" around primarily non-core items. The best negotiators are those who:

⊙ ask all the right questions (the analytics);

⊙ take the best notes (listening and processing skills);

⊙ know what to do with the answers (harvesting knowledge); and

⊙ have the patience and persistence to see things through to the finish line (discipline and result-driven).

Other important skills are having your ego in check. Do not allow negotiation to ever become personal and do not be too quick to prove your intellect at the outset of an encounter. Play a little dumb at first. Observe and listen like a sponge, then react. Ask good questions even if you think you know the answers.

BE READY FOR THE SINK HOLES

A recent headline in The Washington Post read "Discovery of Sinkhole on I-70 Forces Repairs and Disrupts Traffic." The Maryland State Trooper who discovered the sink hole drove over a small bump that was three inches in diameter and barely noticeable to drivers but he was convinced that "something just did not feel right," so he investigated it further. The cause of the small indentation was a sinkhole below that turned out to be 20 feet across and 35 feet deep and could have easily caused life-threatening accidents if left undetected. As you navigate your own path along the road of life, where are your potential sinkholes? On what roads do we travel that appear to be stable but are actually very fragile and on the brink of disaster? On what bridges do we cross that appear to take us to the other side but then collapse when we are only halfway through? Where are the small bumps in your career, your relationships and your health, which if left uninvestigated or undetected could turn into problems, which are much, much larger and even life-threatening? How can we develop the instincts of the Maryland State trooper who went over the bump but then went back because something "did not feel right?" We assume (and often take for granted) that the roads, which we travel in life, are built upon a secure foundation, but we must also build contingencies into our navigational plans to deal with the unexpected surprises and gaps in the road.

CHAPTER 7

DON'T FEAR THE BACK ROADS

"It is not because things are difficult that we do not dare,
it is because we do not dare that things are difficult."

—*Lucius Annaeus Seneca,*
first century
Roman philosopher

"The ultimate measure of a man is not where he sits at times
of comfort, convenience, and consensus, but where he stands
in times of challenge, controversy, and confrontation."

—*Dr. Martin Luther King*
(as adapted)

"Two roads diverged in a wood, and
I took the one less traveled by
And that has made all the difference."

—*Robert Frost,*
"The Road Not Taken"

In the film *Grand Canyon* (one of my favorites), the actor Kevin Kline takes a wrong turn in an attempt to navigate around traffic after a Lakers game and sets into motion a series of events and experiences that will change his life. His navigational blunder leads to a friendship and to a series of revelations that teach him the true meaning of life, and, ultimately, to one of the most awesome places on the earth. He realizes just how minor his problems are when measured against the history and the depth of the Grand Canyon.

When a truck is stuck in traffic, its driver must explore alternative routes based on knowledge, instinct, experience, and of course some satellite-driven, real-time navigational assistance or a radio call into central dispatch. And it is on these back roads where some of life's greatest lessons can be learned. Traffic patterns, construction sites, time of day, and weather all must be taken into account. If we just sit and accept our fate, then yes, we'll eventually reach our destination—but at what cost in terms of the time and productivity lost? And how do we measure the impact of our tardiness?

Trucks are willing to get out of their comfort zone and take risks by exploring alternative paths when necessary. This is not an easy thing to do. People are creatures of habit; it makes most of us uncomfortable when we have to think outside the box and put our security, safety, and comfort at risk. You can learn this skill from watching great NFL quarterbacks. Their instincts and ability to read defenses (and anticipate their next move) in a split-second drives their success. The quarterback who is able to "call an audible" and change direction in mid-play is the leader who is nimble enough to win. Of course, it is a team effort, so when the quarterback changes direction in mid-course, the rest of the team must be in sync. Your decision to change direction on the road of life will often be more effective when you clearly communicate your intent to others, especially those who will be affected by the shift in course.

Trucks also understand the importance of changing lanes from time to time. Getting too comfortable in the same lane leads to complacency and a lack of innovation.

A young boy in a Hummer television ad wins the boxcar race because he goes "off-road" and travels over a few hills to get to the end line. The rules did not state that he had to stay on the road or stay within the white lines, just that he had to be the first to get to the end. His adventurous spirit and sly smile at the finish line say it all: creativity is the fuel along the path to success.

YOU ARE THE DRIVER OF YOUR OWN STRESS MOBILE

I often need to remind myself not to voluntarily put one hundred pounds on my shoulders and then complain that it's too heavy. I must either carry the weight of the world on my shoulders effectively or put it down and let another take that responsibility. But once I agree to shoulder responsibility, I must do so with all my might and absent of martyrdom. If Atlas shrugs, the world collapses—so we must understand the responsibility and accountability that we assume when we decide to emulate him. We will not be able to travel as quickly on the road of life with all of that cargo, but if you don't drop it, you'll have a lot more than others when you arrive at your destination.

SIDE ROADS

It is often on the side roads that we learn the greatest of life's lessons. It was on Walden Pond that Thoreau began to understand the meaning of life. It was on *The Road Less Traveled* that

Dr. M. Scott Peck taught us to seek alternative paths to happiness. It was off the beaten paths and in small sleeping towns that Jack Kerouac shared his most meaningful experiences *On the Road*. It was in the most remote places that James Redfield revealed his deepest insights in *The Celestine Prophecy*. I have always loved all four of these books, not just because they have forced me to rethink my goals and priorities and perspectives, but also because they teach that these inner reflections are more likely to take place when we are far beyond the realms most familiar to us. It may be harder to veer outside of your typical path, but that is also where you may find the greatest rewards.

IMPORTANCE OF PERSPECTIVE

Would you buy a car if it were only equipped with a rearview mirror? Would you invest in a mutual fund solely on the basis that it went up 24 percent last year, even though the SEC mandates a warning that "past performance is not an indication of future success?" Hopefully not. Yet, many of us do exactly that when traveling on the road of life. We live our lives in the past, hoping that previous success will propel future results. It does not work that way. You must be willing to navigate new roads and alternative paths to reach your true destination. The same highways will get you to the same places—every time. As it is often said, "If you keep doing what you are doing, then you'll keep getting what you are getting."

When everyone travels only on the main highways, we share the same limited perspectives and the roads become clogged. Our views are limited to concrete barriers and tree lines, but we never take the time to understand the lives and the communities that thrive beyond the forest. Andre Gide, a nineteenth century French writer, and essayist, once wrote, "One doesn't discover new lands without consenting to lose sight of the shore for a long time." We must have the courage and the conviction to separate ourselves from the familiar to embrace the excitement of the new and unfamiliar.

THE DEATH OF THE DAILY COMMUTE HAS BEEN PREMATURELY REPORTED

"Damn this traffic jam
How I hate to be late
Hurts my motor to go this slow …."
— *"Traffic Jam"*
James Taylor

The impact of modern technology and the high cost of fuel have made telecommuting and flextime popular trends. The ability to be part of a team but also work from home is a very attractive employee benefit and has lead workers from companies like Intel and Hewlett-Packard to relocate to the beaches of Hawaii and the mountains of Colorado, which may be thousands of miles from the crowded cubicle they once called their office. Relief from the daily grind of commuting coupled with online shopping to avoid weekend mall and errand-running traffic could keep all of us off the roads, reducing our dependence on foreign oil prices, congestion, pollution, road maintenance costs and a wide variety of other societal and environmental benefits, wouldn't it? Well, don't be too quick to come to this conclusion. It turns out that people need and want to communicate with other people – what a news flash! In fact, our malls are as crowded as ever, books-on-tape are selling off the shelves and in late 2007, AT&T called back a significant portion of its telecommuters to the daily office grind in order to reassign priorities and realign teams. It turns out that what we really probably need is better public transportation and energy-efficient vehicles, rather than moving towards a society that lacks human interaction and adult conversation.

DON'T CHANGE LANES JUST
FOR THE HELLUVA IT

How many times have you observed another driver changing lanes aimlessly but aggressively only to wind up in the same place and at the same time as you? All of that effort and stress wasted with no net gain or accomplishment of expected result. Many live their life in the same fashion, changing jobs, spouses or hobbies as quickly as they change lanes on the highway, but never really progressing towards their destination any faster or living their lives any happier. We must be open to considering alternative paths and routes, but pursue them for a reason. As my all-time favorite fishing guide Tom Brennan in Battersea, Ontario always advises, "Don't leave fish to find fish." In other words, if there is no good reason to leave the road you are on, don't change lanes or change direction without having thought through the reasons for doing so or with the misperception that an alternative path will get you there any faster.

THE PARADOX OF PROGRESS

We often only take the time to travel the back roads because we have to, not because we really want to—a traffic report advises us of an accident or construction, so in order to avoid delays or stress, we take an alternative path. But it is on that alternative path that we experience new discoveries. We have always had a paradoxical approach towards progress in our society. Everyone wants life to be easy to navigate with plenty of lanes, yet we complain when there is construction to repair and improve the highways. We must learn that there is no progress without delay, no gain without pain. Many times we must move two steps backwards in order to move five steps forwards or take several side roads in order to eventually reconnect with the main road and get ourselves back on track towards a long-term destination. There are many other paradoxes of our age that are well captured in the following thoughts:

THE PARADOX OF OUR AGE

BY DR. ROBERT MOORHEAD

• We have taller buildings, but shorter tempers; wider freeways, but narrower viewpoints.	• We've cleaned up the air, but polluted the soul.
• We spend more, but have less.	• We've split the atom, but not our prejudice.
• We buy more, but enjoy it less.	• We write more, but learn less; plan more, but accomplish less.
• We have bigger houses and smaller families; more conveniences, but less time.	• We've learned to rush, but not to wait.
• We have more degrees, but less common sense; more knowledge, but less judgment.	• We have higher incomes, but lower morals; more food, but less appeasement; more acquaintances but fewer friends; more effort, but less success.
• We spend too recklessly, laugh too little, drive too fast, get too angry too quickly, stay up too late, get up too tired, read too seldom, watch T.V. too much and pray too infrequently.	• We build more computers to hold more information, to produce more copies than ever, but have less communication.
• We have multiplied our possessions, but reduced our values.	• We've become long on quantity but short on quality.
• We talk too much, love too seldom, and lie too often.	• These are the times of fast food and slow digestion; tall men and short character; steep profits and shallow relationships.

• We've learned how to make a living, but not a life.	• These are times of world peace but domestic warfare; more leisure and less fun; more kinds of food, but less nutrition.
• We've added years to life, but not life to years.	• These are the days of two incomes, but more divorce; of fancier house but broken homes.
• We've been all the way to the moon and back, but have trouble crossing the street to meet the new neighbor.	• It is a time when there is much in the show window and nothing in the stockroom.
• We've conquered outer space but not inner space.	• We've done larger things, but not better things.

STRETCH MARKS ON MY SOUL

The back roads hold the keys to creativity and innovation, which are the only way that our society advances and marks our contributions to this world before we leave it. We are likely to be remembered most for our out-of-the-box thinking and unconventional actions than for our "me, too" mindsets and our flights with a large flock. It takes courage to step into the new frontier and travel to the place where breakthrough thinking can take place.

Oliver Wendell Holmes wrote, "Man's mind, once stretched by a new idea, never regains its original dimension." Things must be torn down before they can be rebuilt; they must be tested before they can be improved. We build strength in our bodies by tearing down muscle and allowing it to rebuild even stronger. We build strength in our minds by tearing down the walls of our perceived limitations and allowing them to swim into uncharted waters.

CHAPTER 8

BE AN ALL-WEATHER DRIVER

"Success comes not to those who are willing to walk
only on the flat and wide paths on a comfortable day
with plenty of food and water, but to those who are
willing to walk the windy and narrow path in all
types of weather and with inadequate resources."
—*The Killing Fields*

"The height of your accomplishments will
mirror the depth of your convictions."
—*Unknown*

Being the truck means learning to drive on the road of life in all weather conditions. **I have met many people who always seem to radiate when the sun is shining, but you would not want to hitch yourself to their wagon in a snowstorm.** The skills and discipline to understand how adverse weather conditions affect your path in life are critical to both survival and success. When the going gets tough, the tough get going. You will not always have a warning sign when weather conditions change quickly, and you will need to adjust your driving style accordingly. Living in Washington, D.C., I can be driving my convertible home on the beltway under a sun-filled sky one minute and be scrambling to find a place to pull over to put my top up as a large black cloud approaches the next. The ability to adjust your driving skills and the characteristics of your vehicle to current weather conditions is also a metaphor for how you need to live your life. We put snow tires or even chains on our vehicles to adjust to snow and ice in harsh winters and then take them off when spring approaches. What adjustments do you need to make to your outlooks, perspectives, and actions as weather conditions or seasons in your life change?

The successful people that I know and respect are durable and flexible. They avoid "one-trick ponyism" and pay careful attention to weather and road conditions, adjusting accordingly. They understand how to reinvent and reposition themselves without losing touch with their core values or integrity. They instinctively know when it is okay to drive faster on a clear and open road and when to slow down to navigate an icy downhill path. Others seem to have been built to move at only one pace—they travel at high speed and eventually crash and burn, or move too slowly and let opportunities pass them by. Others carry cargo that is either too far ahead of its time or that is stale, rotten, or obsolete by the time it reaches its destination.

To say that someone is "built like a truck" does not necessarily refer to size; rather it is a testament to their durability—a statement as to how well the person can sustain a body blow and keep on fighting. The durability of a person's success is measured by how well she performs in both good times and bad, how well she can react and regroup after an unexpected loss, an unexpected shift in career, or an unexpected physical or mental challenge. The truck builds deep relationships to gain the strength that it will need to get through the storm, but the roadkill never sees what hit it.

DRIVING IN NEUTRAL

Many of us live our lives as if we were driving in neutral. We can rev up the engine, but the energy created by stepping on the pedal moves us neither forward nor backward. We step on the accelerator, but we are not really going anywhere. How many times has your fear of risk, your desire to be "politically-correct" or not challenge authority impeded your forward (or backward) progress? How many times has a neutral acceleration prevented any real progress or revelation? We must strive to live our lives differently than a hamster on a wheel, expending plenty of effort but failing to make any headway. We must develop the tools and instincts to be able to separate activity from results. ***Our level of energy expended should be roughly parallel to the degree of our progress.***

THE PRICE YOU PAY

The cost for the fuel for our bodies and the fuel for our cars has been steadily rising and it is starting to influence our behaviors in a meaningful way. If we learn to live with a bit less food and dine-out more selectively, it will have a positive impact on our waistlines and our pocketbooks. As to our vehicles, the price for getting to one point to the other has spiraled so far out of control that we are postponing or changing our vacation plans, changing our commuting patterns, carpooling, using more public transportation, moving closer to our workplace, telecommuting, and buying more fuel efficient vehicles. We are driving less but doing more. In 2007, Americans drove a total of less miles than they had the year before – the first time since 1980. So are we going less places or are we finding more efficient and effective ways to get to where we need to go? How can we adapt and apply those same lessons and behaviors on our travels down the road of life? How can we learn to achieve more but consume less? How should the cost of getting from one place to the next influence our path and our pace? How can the cost of being further away bring us all closer together?

BE A DECISIVE DRIVER

> *"You can never win or lose if you don't run the race."*
> —*"Love My Way"*
> **Psychedelic Furs**

Being the truck and not the squirrel depends on your willingness to be *decisive* as part of your commitment to being an all-weather driver. Trucks have drivers that are willing and able to make decisions fairly quickly and to be accountable for the results of their decisions, good or bad. They neither make decisions too quickly nor vacillate until it is too late. They are trained to understand the consequences of their actions (or inactions). They are not afraid to make decisions even if they do not yet have all of the information that they would like to have to feel completely comfortable. They refuse to suffer from "analysis paralysis." Colin Powell said, "If you have less than 40 percent of the information you need to make a decision, then it is probably too soon. If you have more than 70 percent, it is probably too late." General George S. Patton said, "A good plan passionately executed today is far and away better than a perfect plan tomorrow." These were both generals who understood the difference between losing a battle <u>vs.</u> winning the war. Being a truck demands that your decision-making systems (*who* makes decisions, *how* they are made, *when* they are made, and *what* adjustments are made in response to road blocks) must allow for—and tolerate—lost battles as long as the long-term focus is on winning the war.

SLIPPERY WHEN WET

God only knows

God makes his plan

The information's unavailable

To the mortal man

We work our jobs

Collect our pay

Believe we're gliding down the highway

When in fact we're slip slidin' away

Slip slidin' away

Slip slidin' away

You know that you are nearer to your destination

The more you're slip slidin' away...."

—*"Slip Slidin' Away"*
Paul Simon

In our travels down the road of life, we will encounter winter driving conditions (some of us more than others). There is no safe speed when driving on snow and ice. Every stretch of highway will appear different depending on the time of day, the temperature, the severity and intensity of the snow, the angle of the sun, the degree of salting and road treatment, etc.—but **you can be assured that it will be dangerous**. You will need to adjust your driving style and provide more space between you and the other drivers. You will need to start slowing down sooner before you come to an intersection or make a turn. You will need to keep special supplies on hand in the event that you get stuck or the weather intensifies. You must take the time to get a feel for the roadway and test your brakes from time to time to find out how well you can stop. Your critical fluids—anti-freeze, gasoline, oil, and windshield wiper fluid should all be filled to capacity. And just like the lyric from the Paul Simon song above, winter weather conditions may mislead you into thinking that you are reaching your destination faster than you really are and that the closer you get, the more elusive it really is. There is a difference between moving forward and just spinning your wheels in snow or ice. You may be applying the same pressure to the accelerator but your wheels are just turning in place.

Think about the challenges and situations in your life that are akin to driving in snow and ice. Have you adjusted your driving style in the past? Will you next time? Or did you skid out of control, with your driving wheels losing traction on the pavement, only to glide left or right but certainly not forwards?

The ***Maryland Driver's Handbook*** offers this tip to avoid and prevent skids in adverse weather conditions: "Avoid abrupt changes in speed or direction. Drive as though you have an egg between your foot and the gas or brake pedal. When road conditions are bad, leave more time to arrive at your destination." Wow, two great pieces of advice for our navigation down the more challenging segments of the road of life.

Be an all-weather driver. Know how to adjust your speed and style to the road conditions which lie ahead. Plan. Prepare. Adjust. Keep moving forward, not side-to-side. Don't get caught driving too fast or too hard on a surface with thin ice. Take a deep breath and take a few minutes to absorb the wisdom (and the subtle warning) of Jethro Tull from their song *Skating Away on the Thin Ice of a New Day*:

> *Meanwhile back in the year one,*
> *when you belonged to no one,*
> *you didn't stand a chance, son,*
> *if your pants were undone.*
> *'Cause you were bred for humanity*
> *and sold to society.*
> *One day you'll wake up*
> *in the present day*
> *a million generations removed from expectations*
> *of being who you really want to be.*
> *Skating away, skating away,*
> *skating away on the thin ice of the new day.*

So as you push off from the shore,
won't you turn your head once more
and make your peace with everyone?
For those who choose to stay,
will live just one more day
to do the things they should have done.
And as you cross the wilderness,
spinning in your emptiness:
you feel you have to pray.

Looking for a sign that the universal mind has written you
into the passion play.
Skating away, skating away,
skating away on the thin ice of the new day.

And as you cross the circle line,
the ice-wall creaks behind
you're a rabbit on the run.
And the silver splinters fly
in the corner of your eye
shining in the setting sun.

Well, do you ever get the feeling that the story's too damn real
and in the present tense?
Or that everybody's on the stage, and it seems like you're the
only person sitting in the audience?
Skating away, skating away,
skating away on the thin ice of the new day.
Skating away, skating away, skating away…

I will leave it to you, a quiet place, and a glass of wine to extract all of the insights out of this song.

LONG-DISTANCE DRIVING

Life is a marathon, not a sprint. ***Pace yourself.*** You can have a "really bad hair day" and the beauty in life is that you get to wake up the next day and start anew. Each day represents another leg in your journey—a chance to make up ground lost the day before or kick back just a bit because yesterday was so productive. Incremental forward motion is the key, but progress is messy; it does not happen in equal portions, and not each day of each week will not always represent one-seventh of your progress towards your destination. The ability to drive long distances to make up for your pit stops is a critical skill, but not at the expense of others on the highway once inevitable fatigue kicks in. Fatigue is more likely when you push yourself too hard on a long-distance leg of your journey.

Consider another section of the *State of Maryland New Driver's Handbook* on fatigue and driving:

FATIGUE:

Driving for long distances may make you drowsy or unaware of what is happening. Being drowsy is the first stage of falling asleep. Being unaware of what is happening is known as "highway hypnosis." It is caused by monotony—the sound of the wind, the tires and steady hum of the engine. Take these precautions to avoid highway hypnosis.

- At the first sign of drowsiness, do something positive. Don't just sit there and try to fight it.

- At the first rest or service area, pull off the highway and either take a nap, stretch a bit, take a break, or, if possible, change drivers.

- Don't depend on "stay-awake" drugs. They are apt to make your driving even more hazardous.

- Keep the interior of the car as cool as possible.

- To overcome highway hypnosis, make an effort to stay alert.

- Keep shifting your eyes from one area of the roadway to another, near and far left and right. Avoid staring straight ahead.

- Shift your position in the seat.

- Talk to your companion or listen to the radio.

- Vary your vehicle's speed slightly from time to time.

There are some pretty effective tips to be taken from the list above. Highway hypnosis caused by monotony—hmmm, sound like the life of anyone you know? Maybe a little fresh air or a new perspective will wake you up!

RECOGNIZE EBBS AND FLOWS

"There is a tide in the affairs of men
Which, taken at the flood, leads on to fortune;

Omitted, all the voyage of their life

Is bound in shallows and in miseries."

—*William Shakespeare*
(from Julius Caesar)

Every living system is in constant flux. To survive, we must be ready to respond to inevitable change. It is natural for there to be an ebb and flow in relationships, career paths, energy levels, etc. The key is to recognize the ebb as soon as possible and engage the flow to make any adjustments necessary to stay on the path. Engaging the flow is possible when we are centered in our own energy and communicating openly with others (without a hidden agenda). We must have the capacity and the vision to recognize the ebbs and flows of life by:

- ⊙ keeping alert for coincidences and messages

- ⊙ asking questions and acting from inner guidance

- ⊙ always being willing to speak the truth

- ⊙ keeping energy levels high through interaction with nature and other people

- ⊙ growing and evolving, perceiving the world as it really is—a place to learn. There are many new windows of wisdom available to be studied

GOOD DRIVING CAN BE HABIT-FORMING

Aristotle said, "We are what we repeatedly do. Excellence, then, is not an act, but a habit."

I am not going to devote a lot of text to the importance of habits in *Road Rules*® since the Coveys have that market already cornered. What I will say is that good driving along the road of life is not something you just wake up one morning and do. It takes years of practice. You must be patient. Not all lessons can be learned in one day. Excellent habits are formed over time. As Eugen Herrigel teaches us in *Zen in the Art of Archery*, "Steep is the way of mastery. Between the stages of apprenticeship and mastership there lies a long and eventful process of learning and untiring practice."

Herrigel urges us to find the spiritual dimension in the most ordinary of our tasks. Herrigel describes Zen in archery as follows:

> "The archer ceases to be conscious of himself as the one who is engaged in hitting the bull's-eye which confronts him. This state of unconscious is realized only when, completely empty and rid of the self, he becomes one with the perfecting of his technical skill, though there is in it something of a quite different order which cannot be attained by any progressive study of the art...."

After years of practice, a physical activity becomes effortless both mentally and physically, as if the body executes complex and difficult movements without conscious control from the mind.

Our character determines our destiny, our destination. Our character is a composite of our habits, which are essentially an intersection of three critical components: **knowledge** (what we do and why we do it), **skill** (how we do it), and **desire** (our motivation for doing what we do). A commitment to being a good driver along the road of life depends on our abilities to commit to the habit of building strong character and the ability to drive well when road conditions are challenging.

CHAPTER 9

ACCIDENTS CAN HAPPEN EVEN TO THE BEST DRIVERS

"That which does not kill me will only make me stronger."
—Nietzsche

Accidents are the necessary evil of both life and driving. We cannot live our lives without making a mistake, and we cannot get behind the wheel without the chance of a collision. Each year, more than forty thousand people are killed in motor vehicle crashes and over three million people are injured in approximately six million accidents in the United States each year. Research indicates that in more than 50 percent of all crashes, **driver inattention** was a significant factor. How does driver distraction impact performance? Studies show that a focused driver makes approximately two hundred decisions for every mile of driving. If you take your eyes off the road even for three to four seconds at fifty-five miles per hour, your vehicle travels the length of a football field. That means dozens of decisions were not made due to inattentiveness—an accident waiting to happen.

What factors contribute to driver inattention? First, the obvious ones—alcohol or drug abuse, fatigue, reading a map or newspaper, weather and traffic decisions, putting on makeup or shaving, cell phone or PDA use, eating, drinking, smoking, changing radio stations or CDs, retrieving unsecured objects or cargo, focusing on a child or passenger in the back seat, etc.

We have all seen these activities going on in other cars—or our own—on a daily basis. Less obvious factors include mentally focusing on a tough business or family problem while driving, overall stress or anxiousness, running late to an appointment, engaging in an intense conversation, swerving suddenly to avoid an object or person in the road, or driving an unfamiliar vehicle or on unfamiliar road.

So what can we learn about our journey on the road of life from these driving observations? Well, if we are distracted and not focused on the task at hand, then we are significantly more likely not only to fail, but also to hurt others along the way. Syrus, a Latin writer of maxims, once wrote, "To do two things at once is to do neither." We must recognize that by doing multiple tasks at the same time, we increase the likelihood of one or more of these tasks not being done properly or missing important details. Even the most talented jugglers will drop a ball. The key is how quickly you are able to recover and get the object back into the rotation without breaking it. How many times a day are you engaged in a conversation with someone or in a meeting while also answering an e-mail on your PDA, only to find later that you missed something important in the meeting or included something in the e-mail that you now regret? My favorite are the meetings with six to eight participants in which everyone is only half-listening as we all deal with our e-mail and cell phone calls—a gathering not likely to lead to maximum productivity or results.

Should we accept the fact that we are all now "distracted or inattentive drivers," on the road of life increasing our chances of mistakes, failures, and collisions with others as a result of our lack of focus? Or should we seek to strike a greater balance between our ability and capability to multitask with a need to avoid allowing football fields' worth of information and experiences to pass us by? Only you can decide, but there are some lessons from the road worth considering.

Trucks shift into a lower gear for greater control and to slow down their pace when facing a steep decline. There is a business and life lesson in this practice for all of us. When a steep downward hill is approaching, there are steps we can all take to slow the pace and navigate our way to a softer landing. Failure to do so means that the intensity and the pace of the downhill trend will only be that much faster and the impact that much more painful. What are you going to do when your brakes fail? What/where/who is your runaway truck ramp (safety net)?

DARKEST BEFORE THE DAWN

Highway patrol statistics over the years have demonstrated that the greatest number of non-substance abuse related accidents happen during dusk. At dusk, it is not clearly night or day and many of us have trouble adjusting our vision and perspective as a result. We are able to see more clearly when it is either dark or light, just as we are able to make decisions easier when things are black and white. But things are rarely black and white. Life and business success will be driven by your ability to navigate through the grayness of life without colliding into others, who must operate and live their lives inside the same shades of gray.

The skilled driver learns to make adjustments to his driving styles accordingly.

WHERE YOU STAND DEPENDS ON WHERE YOU SIT

A recent study on automobile safety conducted by Allstate Insurance Company examined the likelihood of an accident broken down on a city by city basis. If you are lucky enough to live in Sioux Hills, South Dakota, then your chances of getting into an auto-related collision are averaging one per 14.8 years, the best in the nation, but if you drive in Washington, D.C., like me, that average drops to a staggering average of one per 5.4 years – pretty scary. What are drivers in South Dakota doing differently than drivers in our nation's capital to be three times less likely to collide with one another? Could it be more patience and less stress, along with a healthy dose of good old-fashioned Midwestern values? Are they just less in a hurry to get to where they are going and therefore more respectful and courteous to others on the road? I am very confident that those same driving habits carry over to how they live their lives and interact with each other in their communities.

LEARNING FROM YOUR MISTAKES

The first step in committing to learn from your mistakes is ***accountability***. If you can't admit that you made a mistake, then it will be impossible to learn from it and to avoid making it again. It is only when you become accountable for your mistakes that you have earned the right to enjoy the rewards that will come from the learning that is produced by making them. Don Shula, the long-time, Hall of Fame coach of the Miami Dolphins, once said, "The superior man blames himself. The inferior man blames others." Another great coach, Bear Bryant of the University of Alabama, said, "If anything goes bad, I did it. If anything goes well, we did it. If anything goes really well, you did it." These pigskin coaching lessons reinforce not only the critical importance of accountability as the first step in learning and growing but also drives home the importance of teamwork and the power of praise. Before turning to the *Road Rules* surrounding learning from your mistakes, let's not forget one more important rule of success—that there is a *right* path and a *wrong* path for arriving at your destination. As Joe Paterno, the football coach at Penn State for many decades, once said, "Success without honor is an unseasoned plate of food—it may satisfy your hunger, but it won't taste very good." Reaching your goals without integrity will blind you into thinking that you have succeeded when in fact you have failed miserably.

Everyone makes mistakes—to err is to be human. It is not usually our errors that get us in trouble, however; it is the way we conduct ourselves after making them. Failure is merely an invitation to try something again; each attempt brings you closer to success *if* you learn from your mistakes and react to your failure with integrity, humility, and perseverance. The four classic tragedies of mistake-making are (a) not allowing yourself to act in fear of making them, (b) not learning from them, (c) making the same mistake twice (or more), and (d) allowing a mistake to destroy your self-confidence or willingness to try again. Praise can be addictive, so many of us will strive to avoid error in search of praise. But if avoiding error means creating barriers to progress and personal growth, then the costs are clearly outweighed by the benefits.

Thomas Edison had many famous quotes, one of my favorites being, "I have *not* failed. I have just found the ten thousand ways that won't work." Edison had a great attitude towards what he defined as failure, and it served him well. Edison was also careful to never "invent for invention's sake." He began each project with the needs of the end consumer firmly in his mind.

Mistakes come in all shapes and sizes—there are big ones and little ones, there are ones that cost you time, ones that cost you reputation, and ones that cost you money. There are those that hurt the feelings of others and those that only hurt your own ego. There are those with legal consequences and those that only violate moral codes. Good judgment comes from experience. Okay then, where does experience come from? Bad judgment. It is one of the great ironies on the road to life: we **must** make mistakes to learn from them. We can only hope that our mistakes are not fatal.

So first, let's distinguish between doing something right <u>vs.</u> doing something wrong. Most of us can easily distinguish right from wrong from a moral perspective or as a member of society, respecting the other drivers on the road of life. It is right to help an elderly person with groceries and it is wrong to take another's life. But as we learned about the dusk, things are rarely so black and white. And even if they are, there are exceptions. What if that elderly person has Alzheimer's, mistakenly thinks that you are stealing their groceries, and has a heart attack? What if you take another's life in a clear case of self-defense of your family? These moral quandaries are beyond the scope of this book, but I share them to remind us of the fuzzy lines between what we all typically define as success or failure. Is a hollow success truly success or is it a failure? Is failure coupled with a deep and meaningful learning experience truly a failure or is it a success? Maybe if we focus on the *experience* and not on semantics, we will get our answers.

MAKING THE "RIGHT" DECISIONS

I have always been intrigued with the various ethical frameworks for decision making. Each of us considers different types of variables when we make decisions that have ethical or adverse consequences. The hardest decisions are called "right vs. right" because we are forced to choose between two actions that are both proper, and yet one righteous position will be adversely affected. For example, say you are a supervisor of ten people and can only afford to allow one to take an extra day of sick leave tomorrow, yet two people have severe and pressing family situations. How do you decide? Not all difficult decisions will afford you the convenience of choosing between something that is clearly right vs. something that is clearly wrong. Ethical decision-making frameworks give you some tools to navigate through tough decisions. Here are the five classic frameworks:

   a. The Rights Approach—The rights of those affected by my decision or actions are paramount and should drive my final choice. In this case, you would excuse the worker whose absence will have the greatest impact on their ability to help their family.

   b. The Virtue Approach—My decisions and actions need to be guided by a "do good above all else" principle and should be consistent with a set of ideal virtues. In this case, your decision would be driven by your own sense of ethics, values, and work ethic.

c. Fairness or Justice Approach—My actions or decisions should be driven by principles of fairness above all else—fairness, justness, and equality of treatment of all others must be paramount. In this case, you would allow both to be absent and make other arrangements.

d. Common Good Approach—The benefit of my society, my company, my country, or my neighborhood/community is what needs to come first. If a given action or decision is beneficial for the whole, even if it hurts a few individuals, then it is justified. In this case, you would allow the worker whose absence would have the least impactful effect on other workers to be absent.

e. Utilization/Pragmatic Approach—The costs and benefits of each action or decision need to be carefully weighed; if the benefits of the proposed action outweigh the costs, then action should be taken. In this case, you would carefully weigh the absence of each worker against the costs to the company of their absence, and the impact of not allowing them a day off on future motivation and productivity.

SUCCESS VS. FAILURE

Breathe in deep and read the following thoughts regarding success and failure:

> *"Adversity does not build character, it reveals it."*
> —*Dr. Martin Luther King*

*"Failure isn't so bad if it doesn't attack the heart.
Success is all right if it doesn't go to the head."*
                                    —*Grantland Rice*

*"Judge your success by what you had to
give up in order to obtain it."*
                                    —*Dalai Lama*

*"Life shrinks or expands in proportion
to one's courage and humility."*
                                    —*Anais Nin*

"Success is forgotten long after failure is remembered."
                                    —*Unknown*

*"The accomplishments that made you a hero one
day can make you a goat the next day. Do not
ride too long on the coat tails of your previous
successes before they become ancient history."*
                                    —*Andrew J. Sherman*

The key messages above revolve around the importance of never taking your successes or your failures for granted or allowing your perceptions of success or failure define you as a person. **In your greatest strengths lie your biggest weaknesses and in your biggest weaknesses lie your greatest strengths**. In my life, I have always tried to maximize my strengths and compensate for my weaknesses. But who defines these traits and how sure am I that my perceptions of my strengths and weaknesses are truly aligned with reality—or how others may perceive them? How many of you have pulled up beside another car at what seems like an eternal traffic light only to be entertained by another driver that actually thinks that they are a great singer and you should be blessed to be their audience for the next forty-five seconds? And how many times have you avoided doing something that you have always thought that you were inept, only to find that you excelled?

As humans, we are all guilty of defining parameters around what we consider to be good or bad, success or failures on strengths and weaknesses, all without going through the exercise of testing these premises on beliefs against reality or trying things at least once to see if what we believe about ourselves is even really true. Remember that the definition of insanity is doing the same things over and over again and expecting different results. Step outside the boundaries that you have set for yourself, at least a few times a year, and see if the high jump peg can be moved up a few notches. I think you'll be pleased with the result of the exercise.

Want proof? Try the following at home:

Ask your spouse or child to point to the place on the wall that represents the highest that they perceive that they can jump, and then tape a five-dollar bill to that spot. No surprise, they will jump to that spot and snatch up the five bucks. Now tape a one-hundred-dollar bill three inches above that mark. Do I need to tell you what "magically" happens?

There are countless stories of people that overcame their perceptions of the limits of their ability when tested. The one-hundred-pound woman that lifts up a car to save a child, the person afraid of heights that takes sky-diving lessons on a ten-thousand-dollar wager from a friend—we all just need the motivation to be tested and step outside the very boundaries that we define for ourselves. When we do, we learn. Even if we "fail" when we do, we still learn. And we must learn to evolve, to grow, to prosper, to reach our destination.

CAN YOU AVOID ACCIDENTS?

The surest way to avoid accidents is to never get behind the wheel. You won't travel very far in the road of life, but hey, you'll be safe. But we can't live our lives in fear of a collision or we'll never leave our living room sofas. Coaches teach us that "quitters never win and winners never quit." Getting behind the wheel each day means assuming the risk that we may not reach our destination without a confrontation, a crash, or some pain. We accept this risk as a cost of the reward of eventually getting where we want to go, and we develop stronger armor for dealing with life's adversities during our journey. But we must also know when to use the exit ramp. Quitting while you are ahead is not the same as quitting; before you have made a real effort there is a discipline and a balance that must be learned.

So, if we are incapable of eliminating risk, can we mitigate it? The comforting and resounding answer is **yes**. How can we significantly reduce the chance of an accident as we travel along the road of life?

(a) <u>Focus</u>—Alcohol and drugs are the usual culprits
in driving-under-the-influence (DUI) or driving-

while-intoxicated (DWI) accidents. Our ability to focus is impaired and our judgment is weakened by the substances in our bodies. We put our own lives and selfishly the lives of others at risk when we get behind the wheel in this condition.

When driving along the road of life, excess and abuse of just about anything can also put us and others at risk. Everything in moderation is good advice, whether we intend to "drive" in a few hours or not. We almost need a watchdog group like Mothers Against Drunk Drivers (MADD) to govern our behavior while driving down the journey to our life's destination. Come to think of it, I guess that would just be our mothers![2]

(b) Out-of-State Plates—At the risk of sounding xenophobic, be wary of out-of-state drivers. Whenever I am driving along the road, minding my own business, and spot an out-of-state license tag, my awareness radar goes up two notches! Why? Well, it's not because I assume that drivers from other states were not trained properly. It's just that when they are in my neighborhood, they are out of their element and more likely to cause an accident. Out-of-town drivers are more likely to be lost or clueless

---

2 If you are inspired by this road rule, feel free to start your own local chapter of Mothers Against Children Who Do Not Call Often Enough (MACWDNCOE) or Mothers Against Children Who Do Not Follow Their Advice (MACWDNFTA). I am sure that you will have *a lot* of fellow members!

or distracted, looking at a map or on the phone getting directions. As a result I always want to keep my distance and stay more alert. The life lesson here is not to avoid making contact with people that are not familiar or hail from elsewhere—in fact they are more likely to need your help—but rather to understand that when we are in unfamiliar circumstances, we are more likely to collide with others as we try to find our way and get comfortable.

(c) <u>PDA = Put the Device Away</u>—Our electronic devices have become an extension of our bodies in this modern age. We text message, e-mail, listen to music, and talk on our cell phones while driving, in the bathroom, during meals with family or friends, and even in the middle of meetings or in mid-conversation with another human. The problem is getting worse by the day. Naturally, playing with these devices while driving—no matter how important we think it may be or how confident we are that we can multitask—significantly increases our chance of a car accident. But beyond the highways, this also increases the chance of a collision in life. We half-speak, half-listen, and half-concentrate in meetings, meals, and even during intimate discussions. We leave half the information on the table when we are only half-focused on the task or dialogue at hand. We have become a world of multitaskers, who are jacks-of-all-trades but masters of nothing. We need to learn to focus, to re-connect, to have "naptime" for our PDAs before this problem turns into a crisis.

(d) <u>Read Your Owner's Manual</u>—Be honest. Did you read your owner's manual from cover to cover when you first bought your car? And even if you did, have you read it recently? Are there some things about your vehicle that could help you avoid an accident if you ever took the time to understand them? What if life came with an owner's manual? Would you read it? What if the table of contents took you through the steps for a safer and more efficient way to manage the operation of your life and to achieve your goals? Would you just stick it in your glove box to collect dust?

(e) <u>Have The Right Radio Pre-Set Buttons</u>—The likelihood of accidents on the road of life can sometimes be predicted by a quick audit of the pre-set buttons on your car radio dial. Do you listen to news, weather and traffic reports to be better prepared to understand what is happening in the world around you? Or do you selfishly tune-in immediately to loudly blasting rock'n'roll or hip-hop to tune-out the world? It is probably true that we are all guilty of tuning-in to WIFM (What's In It For Me) radio a bit too often, but some of us are capable of switching to less self-centered stations to avoid collisions. But here's an interesting question to ponder: Do you tune-in to WIFM at the start of the day, expecting to be rewarded from the moment you wake up? Or do you at least wait to tune-in at the end of the day, to wait until you have proven yourself or accomplished something before asking what you get out of a given situation?

AUTOMOBILE INSURANCE AND ACCIDENTS

Most responsible drivers purchase automobile and collision insurance not to prevent accidents, but to mitigate their pain when and if they happen. The rates that you pay are directly tied to your track record of safe driving and you are rewarded for acting responsibly. Your actions dictate and predict a pattern of behavior which reduces the risk of a claim and your costs of coverage are lowered. How can we replicate this system in our society overall? How can we better reward those who are careful not to harm others and reduce their burden for safe passage along the road of life? How can we confer "good driver" benefits to our teachers, our community leaders, our non-profit managers and our civil servants who work tirelessly for the benefit of others?

THE IRONY OF AIRBAGS

If an accident can't be avoided, even by the best and safest driver, there are ways to mitigate the damage from the accident to you and your passengers as well as your vehicle. Wearing seat belts and having a full array of airbags throughout the car and a substantial amount of steel around you will help soften the blow. Yet as comforting as that sounds, the irony is that the deployment of the airbag can cause almost as much damage to your body as the accident itself. Crime and traffic scene investigators often report broken bones, facial injuries, eye injuries (especially if you drive with glasses), and an array of head and neck injuries from the impact of the airbag. While these devices clearly save lives and meet all of my pragmatic benefits, "outweigh the costs" analysis, we ought to be able to design systems that are less harmful.

Airbags are not alone in this ironic category. My car came equipped with the "safer" run flat tires, but like many others, I replaced them because they yielded a very bumpy ride. **That which is safer is not always better; things intended to heal can also harm.** We are strongly encouraged by doctors and personal trainers to engage regularly in exercise (which I support 100 percent), yet I have many friends fighting through their back, neck, knee, elbow, shoulder, shin, foot, and ankle pains from their activities as weekend warriors and unprepared marathon runners. Many cancer treatments—primarily the chemotherapy cocktails—wreak more havoc on the body than the underlying cancer that it seeks to treat. My father-in-law, Max, was in better health and lead a more enriched life living with his cancer than he did when he was being treated with chemotherapy that nearly killed him—and this is a man who survived the Holocaust.

The converse also seems to be true: we are told to avoid alcohol and sugar until a series of studies demonstrates that red wine and dark chocolate (in moderation of course) are high in antioxidants. We are told to avoid caffeine until a study shows that two to three cups per day can actually help fight stress, heart disease, and colon cancer. We are told to avoid red meat, yet many of today's most popular diets favor protein over carbohydrates.

The reality is that our genetics (which we cannot control), our outlook on life and happiness, and our overall mental health and metaphysical wellness (which we *can* help influence and control) have as much to do with our longevity as does our physical health or our proclivity towards dangerous accidents. Recent studies indicate that things like how often we smile or laugh each day, how healthy our family relationships are, and how many people we can count as true friends all influence how long we may live and the quality of our lives along the way. Simplicity is better than complexity. Staying engaged and challenged is better than being dormant or complacent. Being part of the fabric of society is better than being an island. Having people that you love and that unconditionally love you back are all contributors to your health and welfare as well as your ability to confront the adversity that will inevitably and eventually pay you a visit.

DRIVING INTO A WALL

Each year, 32,000 people take their own lives in the United States – that's 80% more than the number of homicides in our nation. Imagine the pain, suffering and anguish that a driver must be feeling before making a decision to voluntarily drive themselves into a wall. Less than 20% of all suicides are on a whim, which means that 25,000 "drivers" each year take the time to plan their own demise. We are only as strong as our weakest link. What can we all do to help these drivers get on the right path and re-connect with the joys of daily driving?

BAD WINS AND GOOD LOSSES

Even something as basic as a win or a loss in an athletic contest offers an opportunity for insight into the need to understand the distinctions of success and failure and the shades of gray that come with the territory. Take a look at this simple coaching matrix and think about how it applies to your life and to the assessment of your accomplishments.

GOOD LOSS	GOOD WIN
BAD LOSS	BAD WIN

- ☉ Good win   The team achieved its goals and took a commendable path for getting there.

- ☉ Bad win   The team reached its intended destination but there is still much to learn as to how it got there.

- ☉ Good loss   The team did not achieve the result it was looking for but did learn how to more effectively harvest their strengths for the next game.

151

⊙ <u>Bad loss</u> Neither the result nor the
path presented opportunity
for team learning or a sense of
accomplishment.

LUCKY IN LIFE? / LUCKY AT DEATH

You may be lucky enough to know when your day comes, and it will hopefully come as no surprise. Be ready for it, embrace it, and be content with the accomplishments, relationships, and other things that you have accumulated for which you can be proud—no regrets, no woulda/shoulda/couldas or resentment towards the life you could have had if only this thing or that thing could have played out differently. It is what it is and it was what it was, so deal with it, accept it, and at the point of your departure it will be too late to change it! Things do tend to happen for a reason; it is too easy to be jealous of another because you think they got dealt a better hand. People show up at the right place and at the right time because they positioned and planned to be there and things worked out in their favor. Former University of Texas football coach Darrell Royal is credited with a quote that has become almost a universally-accepted pragmatic definition of luck. He said, "Good luck is what happens when preparation meets opportunity." Great words to live and die by.

History is likely to remember you as you deserve to be remembered. But have you set the right priorities as to the shaping of your legacy? Have you placed perameters around the ways in which you want those who must live on to recollect your words, your actions, your spirit and your deeds? Have you said what needs to be said and done what needs to be done? Is there unfinsihed business to be accomplished or loose ends which need to be tied? How deep is your "bucket list" of things you still want to experience or places you want to visit?

At the end of the day, it is really about love and how those closest to you choose to keep you in their hearts. The lyrics of the recently deceased songwriter Warren Zevon really capture the essence of my message here in remarkably beautiful prose:

Keep Me In Your Heart
Warren Zevon and Jorge Calderón

"Shadows are falling and I'm running out of breath
Keep me in your heart for awhile

If I leave you it doesn't mean I love you any less
Keep me in your heart for awhile

When you get up in the morning and you see that crazy sun
Keep me in your heart for awhile

There's a train leaving nightly called when all is said and done
Keep me in your heart for awhile

Sometimes when you're doing simple things around the house
Maybe you'll think of me and smile

You know I'm tied to you like the buttons on your blouse
Keep me in your heart for awhile
Hold me in your thoughts, take me to your dreams
Touch me as I fall into view
When the winter comes keep the fires lit
And I will be right next to you

Engine driver's headed north to Pleasant Stream
Keep me in your heart for awhile
These wheels keep turning but they're running out of steam
Keep me in your heart for awhile."

CHAPTER 10

OBJECTS IN THE REARVIEW MIRROR ARE CLOSER THAN THEY APPEAR

"Skate not to where the puck is or was, but rather to where the puck is going."
—*Wayne Gretsky*

O ne of the best NHL players to ever play hockey was Wayne Gretsky (hence, his nickname as "The Great One"). When asked by reporters and other players to explain the keys to his success and ability to score, the quote above was his answer. What he may not have realized at the time is that this lesson and strategy is also a critical component to surviving and thriving in the competitive world beyond the hockey arena. Gretsky understood that the <u>obvious</u> place is not always the <u>right</u> place to be—that things are not always as they seem and that we must not always make our decisions around current circumstances but also lean slightly forward into the future. Trucks understand and embrace the warning that is now mandatory on all vehicles: **"Objects in the rearview mirror may be closer than they appear!"**

There is a famous parable about a man trapped in a Nazi War Camp during the Holocaust. Each night he would leave the work camp and head into the barracks with a wheelbarrow filled with trash. A suspicious German guard carefully inspects the contents but finds only unusable waste. After about thirty days, the confused guard confronts his Jewish prisoner: "Why, may I ask, do you leave here each night transporting trash?" The prisoner smiles back, "I am not transporting trash, I am stealing wheelbarrows." I have always appreciated the irony of this parable. Things are not always as they appear. The mandatory message on the rearview mirror reminds us always that our competitors and others who would like to pass us by are even closer than the mirror may indicate or that we may realize.

Your job in life is to dig deeper. Wear the hat of the journalist, if you will. Gather all of your facts to support your position or chosen pathway, consider the alternative meaning of all situations, read behind the obvious, and don't be afraid to break out of the pack. Most important, **develop the instincts to know where the proverbial puck is going**. It takes self-confidence to skate to where you believe the puck will be. If you are wrong, you'll look pretty silly in the corner of the rink by yourself. But when you are right, you'll be rewarded with a one-on-one chance for a goal—just you and the goalie with no other defenders to stop you. Taking risks is the only way to drink in the rewards (or take a sip from the Stanley Cup one day.)

We encounter these same opportunities and warnings as we travel along the road of life. Think about the signs: "Caution—Black Ice Ahead," "Warning—Bridge Freezes Before Roadway." In both cases, the signs warn that what looks like a safe road may actually be dangerous, because of the deceptiveness of its normal appearance. As one mentor of mine so aptly put it for me years ago, "Be sure that the light at the end of the tunnel is not a train coming right at you." Things are not always as they appear, no matter how hard we want to believe them to be.

WHEN TO BREAK OUT OF THE PACK

Your challenge is to know when to "go with the flow" and stay with the crowds and when to break out and at what pace. And when you do take the risk of making your move, you still need to apply Kenny Rogers' wisdom in knowing "when to hold'em and when to fold'em." Successful entrepreneurs and leaders that I have met over time do not "fly blindly at three hundred miles per hour into the face of adversity" but rather pace themselves and look for opportunities to pause and assess their situation from time to time. They try to mitigate risk wherever possible.

THE INDY PACE CAR

How do NASCAR® drivers going two-hundred-plus miles per hour only centimeters away from one another avoid colliding at every turn? In part, it is the skill and practice of the drivers and in part is the role of the pace car. Wouldn't it be nice if life came with a pace car, helping us speed up and slow down with the flow of traffic and to better anticipate what lies ahead of us? You can and should establish goals and performance benchmarks in your lives to measure progress and adjust your speed accordingly. Understand the situations in which an aggressive pace will win the day and where a steadier pace is required wherein patience is critical. Impatience can be a great motivator for action, but do not let it drive your decisions, particularly those that have long-term consequences. Be careful not to allow short-term variables to impact team decisions or vice versa. The Talking Heads have a great lyric: "I know that patience is a virtue, but I haven't got the time." I have always appreciated the irony and the truth of these words, but developing the instincts to balance speed and patience is the equivalent of having your own pace car for life. It is often said that the only way to eat an elephant is one bite at a time. To avoid indigestion, this certainly seems like the right way to approach elephant consumption and also remember that there is enough meat to share with others. Keeping it all to yourself will only lead to waste (and a bigger waist!)

A LITTLE YIN AND A LITTLE YANG

The *I Ching* teaches us that change is not only inevitable but should be expected and celebrated. The chances of staying on the same course throughout your life are pretty minimal, especially in our dynamic and ever-changing world. Chaos is a critical part of life itself; it shapes us, teaches us, tests us, and molds us. Life is not a merry-go-round; it is a roller coaster. Physics dictates that for a roller coaster to be functional there need to be just as many hills as there are slopes. You must trust your intuition to navigate all parts of the journey. **The Eastern symbol of the Yin and the Yang reminds us that the seen and unseen are part of the same reality.** You can see both a dark comet swirling in a white sky and a white comet swirling in a dark sky. Neither viewpoint is right or wrong. Both are reality but can only be seen one at a time! And just because you can't see an object in one of your mirrors does not mean it does not exist or that it will not impact you. We often talk about a given car's "blind spots"—those places where you can not see something that is still very much there. Where are your "blind spots"? What other perspectives must you work harder to see and understand before you will truly comprehend the full picture?

These same principles apply to our navigation of the road of life. In most cases, how we react and adjust to the unexpected twist, turns and detours along our paths define us as a person. Our ruggedness, durability, sustainability and persistence when life presents its best and worst surprises will play a large role in determining our pathways to success (and survival). Will you be a hero or a goat when challenged with circumstances beyond your control and which interrupt the smoothness of your journey? Will you have the vision to embrace adversity and find worthwhile solutions? As Albert Einstein said, "Small is the number of them who see with their own eyes and feel with their own hearts. But it is their strength that will decide whether the human race must relapse into the state of stupor which a deluded multitude appears today to regard as the ideal."

CAN WE CREATE FATE?
Benjamin Disraeli said, "We make our fortunes and then we call them fate." Circumstances do not happen by chance or

accident. Our behaviors, our attitudes, and our decisions all shape our success and destinations along the road of life. We can take nothing for granted. We must prepare for adversity in times of prosperity and strive towards prosperity in times of adversity. We are taught to drive defensively. Life can be warfare against the malice or negligence of others; we cannot assume that others on the road have made the same commitments to the habits of safe and effective driving that we have. We cannot rely on the people or objects in our blind spots to know that we cannot see them.

The following parable drives this point home:

A bird is flying south when suddenly it becomes very cold and the snow on its wings causes it to become so heavy that it can no longer fly and falls to the ground. As it lies shivering in the snow, a large elephant comes along and poops on its head, but the warmth of the excrement allows the bird to survive the storm and frigid evening. The next morning a cat comes along and digs the bird out of the heap, and then eats him.

The moral: Not everyone who poops on you is your enemy, and not everyone who pulls you out of poop is your friend.

CHAPTER 11
LIFE IS A FOUR-WAY INTERSECTION

"Seek first to understand if you want to be understood."
—*Stephen Covey*

Why does every eighteen-wheeler in the nation have a sign on its rear that says, "Caution: This Vehicle Makes Wide Turns." The need to warn others on the road and to work in tandem to avoid an accident is a critical aspect of being the truck and not the squirrel. It is important to understand the impact your actions will have on the reactions of others. You have probably heard the expression that 10 percent of life is what happens to you and 90 percent is how you react. This highlights the importance of attitude, awareness, and clear, concise, crisp communications as you travel along the road of life.

LOOK BOTH WAYS BEFORE CROSSING

Consider the dynamics of the four-way intersection. Stop signs and traffic lights are installed to control the flow of traffic and avoid collisions. Your obligation is to approach the crossroad slowly and look both ways before crossing. At a four-way stop sign, the ability to communicate with the three other drivers is critical. It may be unclear who arrived first, who has the right of way, who perceives themselves in the biggest hurry, who is not paying careful attention, who may be confused and lost their

161

way, or who may be just ignorant of the rules of the intersection. You should **assume nothing**. Rely on instinct and your communication skills to guide your way and assure safe passage. Always communicate with the right blend of truthfulness and directness to be counterbalanced by tact and diplomacy.

The upshot? Consider all alternatives and carefully weigh all variables when reaching an inflection point in your life, where decisions need to be reached, the actions of others carefully considered, and the consequences of your choices fully understood. We all travel through dozens if not hundreds of literal and metaphorical four-way intersections per day without ever considering the significance of their existence and the lessons which they can teach us.

Green lights tell us when to go and red lights tell us to come to a complete stop. Going through a red light is dangerous because it's not your turn to move forward. It's your time to pause, reflect, and prepare yourself for the next journey while others have an opportunity to travel on their path. How many of life's red lights have you crossed at the expense of endangering others?

But life usually presents more yellow lights, where the decision to proceed or slow down is not so clear-cut. We often live our lives mired in the shades of gray in between black-and-white decisions, consequences, and actions. When we see the yellow light, we proceed with caution; we do not know precisely when the light will turn to red or how many anxious drivers will accelerate quickly when their light turns to green. If we stop suddenly on a yellow light, we are likely to get hit by the car behind us. If we speed up and go through the light quickly, we run the risk of the light turning red and being hit by another vehicle or receiving a traffic citation. We rely on our knowledge of the intersection, our vision and clarity, our training and experience, our understanding of traffic patterns, road conditions, etc., to help us make this decision in less than one second, dozens of times each day. We are decisive and we accept the consequences of our actions and our choices. We are accountable to others if our decisions cause harm (unless we make the morally corrupt decision of a "hit and run"). Why can't we apply the same approach to the "yellow lights" presented to us in life?

USING YOUR TURN SIGNALS

I wish that humans were programmed with turn signals (I also wish more humans would actually *use* their turn signals in their vehicles—but that's a different problem for another day). How many times has someone you work with or someone you live with changed direction on you, with no communication and without advance notice? Too many of us change our minds like we change lanes—quickly and without regard to the paths (or feelings) of others. When will we all learn that it is perfectly acceptable to change our course in life, but if someone nearby is affected by our actions, then common courtesy would dictate that you give them a "heads-up" so that they can adjust and react? Many of us live our lives in such a blur that we're not always aware of our own motives and desires until they become overwhelming, leaving us little time to alert others? Or we are so focused on our own needs that we don't understand or analyze the consequenes of our actions on others who will be directly or indirectly affected by our actions, our decisions as well as our inaction or indecision. How can we live with more attention to that inner voice, so we don't suddenly foist these changes upon others – and ourselves – with no warning?

COMMUNICATIONS AND ACCOUNTABILITY

What if every car on the road had to have a "How's My Driving?" Call 1-800___-____" sticker on the back bumper? Or if we all had to wear the equivalent of that same sticker on our foreheads, asking "How am I treating you?" Wouldn't that be great? But would it create better drivers if we know that the next time we drove aggressively or cut another off, there was a central repository to report bad driving or rude behavior? Maybe we all need to wear that same sticker on our foreheads! The truth is that in today's inter-connected and socially-networked world we do have better ways to keep each other accountable for our behaviors – good, bad or otherwise. Technology has enabled us to keep tabs more closely on one another and warn others when someone is not following the rules. eBay® allows buyers to rate the integrity of sellers and iTunes® allows music fans to share their views on a new release by today's latest musicians. Integrity is regulated not by a set of humans on Capitol Hill, but rather by each one of us able to communicate in ways never imagined a short ten or twenty years ago. We shouldn't have to have a sticker on our heads to make us treat others well or to create accountability or inspire integrity. We should be policing our own behavior, so others don't have to "call the highway patrol" to complain about a truck driving them off the road or some telephone bank or dispatch to alert an employer that a driver/employee is being inconsiderate. Fear of being caught or reported shouldn't be what motivates us to be better drivers on the road of life.

TWO-WAY STREETS

How many times have you heard the phrase "_____ is a two-way-street." Insert almost any word that is important to you; *respect, love, communication, empathy, happiness*—the wisdom of the phrase still applies. **You get what you give.** If you reach a point on your path where there is doubt or confusion, take the high road! It is the path with the best perspective and the superior moral vantage point. We each must be sensitive to the needs of other drivers and respect the other side of the road, even when we are traveling in different directions. If I cross over the double yellow lines and hit you, we both die in a head-on collision. If you respect my space, we communicate and both follow the rules of the road, then we both get to safely reach our intended destinations. Oh so simple, and yet oh so complicated in practice. Yet if we can do so on the road, why can't we apply those same principles to our lives? The answer is that *we can, we will, and we must.*

RIGHT OF WAY

Highway traffic laws dictate who has the right of way in a given situation—at a four-way stop sign, a traffic light, a yield sign, or an entrance ramp. But who has the right of way in life? She who got there first? He who is the biggest and strongest? She who has the most friends? He who dresses the best? She who whines the loudest? Or he who is committed to doing things properly? **The right of way belongs to those who do things the right way.** Just because you have the right to do something doesn't always make it right to actually do it. Yielding action can be as effective as taking action under the right circumstances. Be guided by what's right, not by what you have a right to do.

<u>Remember always</u>:

- ☉ Your <u>thoughts</u> shape your <u>actions</u>.

- ☉ Your <u>actions</u> shape your <u>character</u>.

- ☉ Your <u>character</u> determines your <u>destiny</u>.

Your ultimate destination on the road of life begins with your thoughts, including your reaction to the actions of others.

SECONDS CAN MAKE THE DIFFERENCE IN THE PIT CREW

In *Sliding Doors,* the actress Gwyneth Paltrow plays a woman whose entire life is different because she boarded a subway car only three minutes earlier than the next train. What happens to her throughout the film is affected by her decision, one that was entirely random and within seconds of an alternative path. In fact, the entire film is intended to remind us of the much larger consequences that can result from the smallest of our decisions, which are made within seconds. Our lives are defined by the consequences of the hundreds of decisions we make each day, the thousands we make each month, and the millions we make in a lifetime.

Think through the consequences of your choices and your attitudes. Take, for example, the story of the master carpenter who tells his employer that he wants to retire. He has been a hard worker, skilled in his trade, but feels that the time has come to end his career. His employer, the owner of the building company, asks the carpenter to complete just one more home. The carpenter reluctantly agrees and takes on his task, using poor workmanship and substandard materials. When the employer arrives to inspect the completed home, he hands the carpenter the keys to the home as a gift for his lifelong services.

You must live with the consequences of your actions, live in the house that you built and sleep in the bed as you made it. If you take on each task with pride and care, then you will reap the rewards of your labor. Fisherman and hunters are often reminded to not lose sight of the journey vs. the end goal in mind. They often say, "Don't get caught up in the thrill of the chase without recognizing the consequences of the catch." This is a good reminder not only to understand the consequences of our actions but also to be careful what you wish for—you might just get it.

A TRIP TO THE CATSKILLS

Two older widows save up all of their money in hopes of going to a very posh resort in the Catskills for the weekend. They finally have enough to go and are excited to sit down for their first meal. After dessert, one turns to the other and says, "You know, the food here is terrible." To which the other responds, "I know, and the portions are so small!"

No matter how miserable life can get, we nevertheless cannot get enough of it.

ATTITUDE IS NOT THE MAIN THING, IT'S THE ONLY THING

Vince Lombardi was famous for sayings like "It's not the size of the dog in the fight, but the size of the fight in the dog," and "It's not whether you got knocked down, it's whether you get back up." He taught his players that attitude can *overcome* skill, ability, talent, resources, and even preparation—it is the ultimate competitive advantage. Attitude is what guides you to your destination with a clear and stress-reduced state of mind. The guy who cuts you off without notice as you head calmly and confidently towards your destination can either be someone that you wish a hex on his family and future generations or can be someone that you laugh off as being an oaf. Rise above the pettiness and you will unlock and liberate an amazing amount of energy that can be allocated to higher pursuits.

Do you know who Bert and John Jacobs are? They took a simple phrase reflecting on attitude—Life Is Good®—and built it from a company selling T-shirts from the back of their van ten years ago into a one-hundred-million dollar per year enterprise and a nine-hundred product line of merchandise ranging from apparel to hats to dog beds. How did this small company establish such a widely-known brand? It was not with huge marketing budgets, the way that Nike or General Motors do; it was quite simply by "tapping into an emotional ethos that struck a chord with where our culture was at a certain point in time," as one of the co-founders aptly put it. Life Is Good® customers became evangelists for the brand and brought it to life by giving it passion, visibility, and credibility. Other small companies have relied on this level of grassroots marketing to establish brand by connecting with our culture at a relevant inflection point, such as Stonyfield Farm® yogurt, Vitamin Water® beverages, or Zipcar® vehicle rentals. From a *Road Rules*® perspective, I share the story of the Jacobs brothers not just because it is reflective of what is so fantastic about our entrepreneurial society—the ability to make something out of nothing—but also to understand the significance of how a simple phrase can impact all of us in different ways and at different times.

Life *is* good. When the company was launched in the late 1990s, our society was caught up in the technology and Internet boom that sent many of our 401(K) accounts into the stratosphere as the NASDAQ hit 5200. But the party came to a rapid halt in March of 2000, and the events of September 11, 2001, only further sent our attitudes into a downward spiral.

Yet, sales at Life Is Good® continued to soar. Why? Because this simple affirmation still carries an important reminder for many of us.

By the way, in 2007 the Jacobs brothers launched Good Karma®, a new line of environmentally friendly clothing. Kudos to them for not falling asleep at the wheel! Never, ever take your personal brand for granted. It must always evolve.

THE ATTITUDE OF OTHERS

You can only control your own outlook, your own perspectives on life, and your own attitude during each situation. Your advice, mentoring, parenting, and actions can hopefully influence the outlooks of others in a positive manner; but the advice or needed life lessons are learned far more effectively when those who need to learn them experience the lessons for themselves and can reach real-time conclusions as to their actions or behaviors. There is no substitute for experience. It is virtually impossible to get a tiger to change its stripes, unless it really wants to do so. As I often tell my family and clients, don't be surprised or concerned when people act consistently with their character. In fact, be more worried when they don't!

We cannot control how others feel or the things that they may say or do to hurt us. We *can* control how we react to them and the gravity with which we treat their remarks. It has been said, "Strong is the man who can build a secure foundation from the bricks and stones that are thrown at him by his adversaries." Our perspective shapes our attitudes; we can choose to see a half-full glass of water as half-full or half-empty. We can choose to scorn the rosebush for having thorns or praise the thorn bush for having roses. It is not a matter of right vs. wrong or truth vs. lies in either scenario; it is only a matter of viewpoint, attitude, and outlook.

When ego, foolish pride, turfmanship, greed, politics, ignorance, or fear are allowed to shape our perspectives, we are more likely to see glasses as half-empty and scorn the rosebushes. We need to check our egos at the door in most situations. If we "cannot be the star of every show, then aim to be the best actor or actress in a supporting role," as Rabbi Harold Kushner has advised in *Living a Life that Matters*. We need to find gratification in doing what we can to help and assist others, even when we are not in the spotlight. Parents, coaches, and teachers understand and accept this role. Watch the Heisman Trophy award program each year (or any awards program), and you will see that each winner takes the time to thank parents, coaches, and teammates, who usually seem as excited (if not even more so) as the winner.

Let's close out this chapter on the importance of communication, perspective, respect for others, and attitude by pondering this great observation by Mark Twain:

"When I was a boy of fourteen, my father was so ignorant I could hardly stand to have the old man around…. But when I got to be twenty-one, I was astonished at how much he had learned in seven years."

CHAPTER 12

DON'T JUDGE A DRIVER BY HIS VEHICLE

*"The purpose of life is not to reach the end in a
pretty and well-preserved body, but rather to skid
in sideways, thoroughly used up, totally worn out
and loudly proclaiming: Wow, what a ride!"*
—Unknown

Trucks are not pretty. Neither is the pathway to success. Drivers along the road of life that are primarily concerned with their vanity will never accumulate the battle scars needed to be considered veteran warriors ... and survivors. Success is not for the vain, the conceited, or those more fascinated with hood ornaments than the performance of the engine.

Similar principles apply to success with athletes. Those willing to risk a dent, scratch, or bruise in exchange for the possibility of reaching their maximum potential are also more likely to work hard and recover more quickly, even stronger than before. You must be willing to sacrifice in order to move your life plan forward in a fashion likely to reach your destination. Few of us learned to ride a bicycle without a few scraped knees and bloody elbows along the way. A game plan for life built solely on material wealth or selfishness, vanity, and ego is just a squirrel waiting to be run over.

How many times have we looked at the car next to us at a traffic light or in front of us on a crowded highway and come to a series of conclusions about the driver? Like the car we drive, we are often judged by others by the clothes we wear, the jewelry we buy, and the house we live in instead of what really matters—the people that we are.

DON'T JUDGE A DRIVER BY THE MAKE OF HER VEHICLE

We are taught as children not to "judge a book by its cover." It is a simple but important message about the importance of peeling back the cover to truly see inside a person, situation, or challenge. Until we peel additional layers of the onion, we do not know whether it is wholesome or rotten at its core. It is also at this core that we can understand the needs of one another and how we can help each other along our paths and towards our destinations. I keep a cutout of a simple piece of business advice first published in the mid-eighteen hundreds taped to my computer screen. It reads, "Help your clients and customers towards a path of building wealth and your rewards will soon follow." To put others first, we must learn the discipline to never judge them until we truly know them, and probably not even then. And we must certainly not judge them by something as petty as the car they drive. Vanity is the enemy of empathy, humility, and sincerity.

We think we know so much about a person from the car they drive, yet we really know so little. Sam Walton drove to his office in Bentonville, Arkansas, everyday in an old pickup truck until the day he died. Warren Buffet drives to work in an old Cadillac. Many of Hollywood's biggest stars drive a Toyota Prius.

Our duty is not to see through one another but to see one another through. Vanity becomes the enemy of empathy, humility, sincerity, and even reality. Our quest for a bigger, faster, or nicer car blinds us to the beauty of the road we need to travel to be in a position to afford such a vehicle. We can never let the end become more important than the means, and we must never allow the means to overtake the importance of the meaning.

In the soundtrack of the film *Into the Wild*, Eddie Vedder pokes fun at this phenomenon and deeply questions our priorities as he sings the song "Society" (written by San Francisco songwriter/singer Jerry Hannon). The lyrics, in part, are as follows:

> *It's a mystery ....*
> *We have a greed to which we have agreed.*
> *You think you have to want more than you need,*
> *And until you have it all, you won't be free.*
>
> *Society, you're a crazy breed,*
> *I hope you won't be lonely without me."*

The main character is a recent college graduate who goes deep into the wilderness to reject his perception of our priorities and in search of personal insights. But in his quest for an understanding of the meaning of life, his pendulum swings too far and he dies in isolation.

We don't need to go quite this far to reject the dark side of greed, vanity, or success at any price. But those who step on a lot of hands and toes to climb the ladder of success ultimately pay the price. This is the core principle underlying karma: **that which goes around comes around**. Devote your life to helping others succeed and you will be successful in many ways and on many different levels well beyond the material things that you can touch, feel, and admire. Dedicate your life to material and financial success at any cost, at any price, and at any speed along the highway of life, and I can assure you that you will miss all of the beauty along the way, eventually either crashing and burning or at the very least being pulled over by a state trooper and cited for "speeding through life" or "reckless operation of your visit to Earth."

FINDING INNER BEAUTY

There are many cars and trucks that are not particularly attractive on the outside but offer many features, luxuries, and comfort on the inside. You spend your time behind the wheel on the interior of the vehicle while only the general public and your fellow commuters look at the exterior of the vehicle. On which should you be focused? Some of us only care what others think of us, no matter how weak or disorganized we may be inside. Others are not as focused on appearance but rather on developing the best heart and mind. If we focus on a strong interior, our exterior will shine to others, irrespective of whether we look like a Mercedes 500 SL or an old Yugo. Sometimes a vehicle is truly broken, but often it just needs a new part or some basic repair. Sometimes our exteriors are truly worn down and rusted out, but often we just need a scratch removed, a dent knocked out, or a fresh coat of paint. Just don't be too fast to judge others by what you see (which is often easily corrected); rather make an informed decision about them based on what you hear and how you feel after you spend time with them.

As we age, if we let vanity define us, then that is a battle which will surely be lost. Focus on inner beauty and accomplishment to define you as a person. Each decade, ask yourself: Am I wiser than I was ten years ago? Have I helped more people today than I did ten years ago? What difference have I made in the lives of others? Am I closer to my next destination? Or has my engine of progress stalled or my path disrupted for distractions which are motivated by vanity or jealousy?

BE CAREFUL WHAT YOU WISH FOR

Children's stories are filled with messages about being careful what you wish for, you might just get it, but lose sight of what is really important along the way. The poor man who wishes for riches and winds up with gold but nobody to share it with. The man who wants to marry the most beautiful girl in the village and winds up in an unhappy relationship for the rest of his life. When we are jealous of others and let our envy be the fuel of our ambitions, we are no longer following our intended paths but fighting to walk in the shoes of another. Envy is the mirror image of vanity. People who are vain lose sight of what's really important in life, but envy perpetuates and accelerates this misguided sense of priorities. Don't let the accomplishments of others define your mission in life or the pace at which you try to reach your destination.

U-TURNS

There is another risk in focusing your life too heavily on vanity, ego, or selfish pride—never knowing when you will voluntarily or involuntarily make a U-turn in your life that has you headed in the wrong direction at an accelerated pace. Most of our turns on the highway of life will be gradual and slight, like the angle of an easy to navigate exit or entrance ramp. At other times, we will knowingly make a right or left turn to navigate at 45 degrees a path towards our destination. Our voluntary U-turns at 180 degrees will be rarer. But the most painful are the involuntary U-turns—the unexpected loss of a job or loved one, an unanticipated and severe health problem, a sudden jolt in the marketplace, a violent storm or a terrorist attack. These U-turns provide the ultimate humility and a recognition of what's truly important—but you do not want to rely on them for a rebalancing of your priorities. Do not wait for disaster to deliver the news as to what is really important in life.

CHAPTER 13

RANDOM THOUGHTS
AND BUMPER STICKERS

*Truckin', got my chips cashed in. Keep truckin', like the
do-dah man*
Together, more or less in line, just keep truckin' on.

Arrows of neon and flashing marquees out on Main Street.
Chicago, New York, Detroit, and it's all on the same street.
Your typical city involved in a typical daydream
Hang it up and see what tomorrow brings.

Dallas, got a soft machine; Houston, too close to New Orleans;
New York's got the ways and means; but
just won't let you be, oh no....

Most of the cats that you meet on the streets speak of true love,
Most of the time they're sittin' and cryin' at home.
One of these days they know they better get goin'
Out of the door and down on the streets all alone.

Truckin', like the do-dah man. Once told me you've got to
play your hand
Sometimes your cards ain't worth a
dime, if you don't lay 'em down,

Sometimes the light's all shinin' on me;
Other times I can barely see.
Lately it occurs to me, what a long, strange trip it's been."

— *"Truckin'"*
The Grateful Dead

Our purpose in life is to acquire knowledge, apply it wisely in order to grow as people, and to "keep on truckin.'" The more wisdom we are able to gather and the things that we do with the knowledge we have accumulated determine the success of our journey in the long, strange trip of life, helping us to evolve into the strongest and most durable vehicles on the highway.

As a citizen of society, your challenge is to gather knowledge from a diverse set of sources, synthesize it, organize it, process it, and use it in ways to build financial and emotional health and to live a life of enlightenment. Successful people learn to (a) *always* stay in a learning mode in which they are open-minded to new ideas, perspectives and insights; (b) recognize that their most important lessons in life and business may not come from the most obvious sources (seminars, books, coaches, etc.) or from the most likely venues; and (c) be sensitive to the fact that insights that may help you grow as a person can and will come from virtually anywhere and at unexpected times—but only if you are open to them and recognize them when they are shared.

Being a truck and not a squirrel means being a road warrior that always has his or her antennae up, mind open and heart ready to receive and process wisdom. Insights and opportunities for improvement may also come from both the obvious (teachers, supervisors, parents, mentors) and the not so obvious (neighbors, former or prospective customers or clients, the guy who sits next to you on an airplane, someone you meet in an elevator, etc., competitors, alliance partners, overseas buyers, academics, etc.). In the television series *Friday Night Lights*, actor Kyle Chandler plays Texas high school football coach Eric Taylor, who tells his players before each game, "Clear eyes ... full hearts ... can't lose!" This is an excellent formula for success: a clear vision for the future and a heart and mind open to learning and growth. Every person, every experience, and every challenge has a message for you, but only if your heart and mind are open to listen and absorb them, and you pause long enough to learn from them.

Being a truck also means understanding your role as a transporter of cargo. You are a catalyst, a person who is committed to being a transporter of knowledge, insights, experience and tools for survival. Define yourself as someone who always carries a cargo of valuable assets with you wherever you go, always ready to pull up to the loading dock and deliver these assets to where they are needed the most. Without you, these assets sit in a warehouse and never reach their intended destination.

Trucks also develop a keen instinct, a set of tools, and a series of filters to distinguish which information and insights may be helpful and which will only confuse things or make matters worse. Attempting to integrate every insight and every bit of information is like trying to "drink a fine cabernet from a fire hose;" you won't get to enjoy any of it and you'll end up only with an expensive dry cleaning bill. The focus should always be on quality, not quantity, when seeking out information that enhances your life. If you take a course or attend a seminar or conference and learn just a few "pearls of wisdom" or "golden nuggets," then the investment of time will have been worthwhile. The higher quality insights are more likely to come to you from a small sip from a cognac or port glass than they are in a Big Gulp® cup. In a society that places value on Jumbotrons, super-sized meals, and triple-patty burgers, it may take some discipline and some attitude adjustment to embrace this insight. Trucks commit to becoming lifelong learners but with the discipline to filter out the inaccurate, inapplicable, and inane.

DRIVING FORWARDS

The other insight to be harvested from the Keep on Truckin' message is the importance of momentum and forward motion. We must keep the wheels of progress and development in our own lives moving forward—inertia is the kiss of death.

You have probably never heard of anyone reaching their destination or winning a race by going in reverse (except of course, Will Ferrell in the film *Talladega Nights*). Trucks survive by understanding that business and life is all about momentum, forward progress, and riding the crest of the wave when the tide is highest. They embrace the Japanese concept of **Kaizen** (e.g. the importance of continual improvement and forward progress). The drivers of trucks understand that you must never stop moving forward, or like the shark, the truck will die. Trucks mimic the path of water in a river, flowing forward in the same direction, seeking the path of least resistance, and getting stronger along the way. U-turns are not a strategic option.

Squirrels often confuse activity with results. If you watch them for an extended period of time, they scamper about and move in many different directions but do not appear to be going anywhere or accomplishing anything. They assume that being swamped means that they are making headway, when in reality they are running hard and fast but in reverse. They are not moving forward enough to pick up the subtle clues that momentum has been lost. Once momentum and focus are lost, they are more likely to be frozen like a deer in the headlights, standing in the middle of the competitive highway just waiting to be hit by a truck!

But even the most successful people need a short "breather" at some point. Choose your rest stops wisely. Know when it is time to use vacation or even sabbatical time to take yourself off the highway for a bit to avoid burn-out, exhaustion, or falling asleep at the wheel.

Remember that success in your career and in life is a marathon and not a sprint. Persistence and a healthy impatience (but not raw speed alone) will get you to your destination in one piece.

BUMPER STICKERS

There is probably no more appropriate way to end my thoughts on the rules for navigating the road of life than with a focus on the tail end, the bumper of the car, the last thing everyone sees as you pass them by or when they are stuck behind you. Bumper stickers give us a chance to share our insights, express our political or policy views, pay homage to our favorite vacation spots or support our local sports teams – but is it possible that they can also define us as drivers?

In June of 2008, the results of a University of Colorado study was published which linked bumper stickers with road rage. The study purported to find that those of us who choose to express our views on the asses of our cars were also more likely to act like asses on the road. The study found that people with bumper stickers on their cars are both more opinionated and more territorial, thereby making them more prone to be enraged if their opinions are questioned or their territory invaded, leading to aggressive behavior on the road. Apparently, even those who place bumper stickers on their cars which preach love, world peace and acceptance of others are significantly more likely to succumb to road rage than those who keep those same thoughts to themselves (or who act on them instead of using these principles as car decoratives). Hmmmm – some interesting observations, (and irony) to consider about those who are always talking about their beliefs vs. those who walk more quietly but act consistently with their core values.

Here are some of my favorite bumper sticker messages for your consideration and enjoyment:

- Follow Your Dreams (Except that One Where You Go to School in Your Underwear)

- A Day Without Sunshine Is Like … Night

- He Who Laughs Last, Thinks the Slowest

- Change Is Inevitable, Except from Vending Machines

- Just Say NO to Negativity

- I Thought I Was Indecisive, But Now I'm Not Sure

- Those Who Discourage Your Dreams Are Likely to Have Abandoned Their Own

- Our Greatest Glory Is Not in Never Falling but in Rising Every Time We Fall (Confucius)

- Don't Make Me Come Down There! (God)

- On the Advice Of Legal Counsel, This Sticker Contains No Message

- We're All in This Thing Together

- If You Observe This Vehicle Being Operated in an Unsafe Manner, Call 1-800-WHO-CARES

- Time Is Nature's Way of Keeping Everything from Happening at Once

- ⊙ If You Can't Laugh at Yourself, Let Me Do It for You

- ⊙ You're So Vain—I Bet You Think this Sticker Is about You

- ⊙ What We Learn from History Is What We Fail to Learn from History

- ⊙ People Would Rather Be Wrong than Be Different

- ⊙ Shut Up and Dance!

- ⊙ Not all who wander are lost

- ⊙ Act as you are, not as others want you to be

- ⊙ Know the difference between people of words and people of deeds

- ⊙ Avoid doing battle with those who have nothing to lose

- ⊙ The harder the conflict, the more glorious the triumph

- ⊙ Judge your success by what you had to give up to get it

- ⊙ Fear is that little darkroom where negatives are developed

- ⊙ What you do is not who you are

- ⊙ What if it turns out that the Hokey Pokey *is* what it's all about?

- If I do not go within, then I go without

- Share with those around you in times of victory, and they will be more likely to support you in times of defeat

- You can only be as happy as your saddest child, your most confused student, or your most distressed neighbor

- A chain is only as strong as its weakest link

- What I Am Not, I Have Learned
  What I've Got, I Have Earned

  -- B. Springsteen

- When the Going Gets Tough, the Tough Get Tougher

- Don't say or do anything in life that you would not want to read about on tomorrow's front page

- Fear of loss is often stronger than the desire for gain

- Success comes to those who focus on their character, not their reputation

- Build it slower and it will last longer

- Strive to be part of the solution, not part of the problem

- Feed your brain every day or it will die of starvation

- ⊙ There is a big difference between being frugal and being cheap

- ⊙ Nothing truly worthwhile is ever easy to achieve

- ⊙ If you can't handle wearing three hats, then you shouldn't have three heads

- ⊙ Passion and determination will always triumph over raw talent

- ⊙ Do it as if your life depended on it

- ⊙ Energy follows thought

- ⊙ <u>What</u> is right is more important than <u>who</u> is right

- ⊙ Don't defer to tomorrow what can (and should) be tackled today

- ⊙ Go with *your* gut—it's the only one you have

- ⊙ People will have a short memory for your achievements and a long memory for your mistakes

- ⊙ Slow Thinkers Keep Right

- ⊙ What Doesn't Kill You Still Requires A Co-Pay

- ⊙ A Poor Memory Is Not the Same as a Clear Conscience

- ⊙ When "It" Hits the Fan, "It" Will Not Be Evenly Distributed

- Even if the Voices Are Not Real, They Have Some Good Ideas

- Make Someone Happy, Stay in Your Own Lane

- Squirrels Are Nature's Speed Bumps

- The Truth Will Set You Free. But First It Will Piss You Off.

- The Winner of the Rat Race Is Still a Rat

- An Eye for an Eye Will Make the Whole World Blind

- The Road to Success Is Always Under Construction

- Be Willing to Give Up What You Are for What You Can Become

- Integrity Has No Need for Rules

- If This Sticker Is Getting Smaller, then the Light Is Probably Green

- Age Brings Wisdom (Or Shows Up Alone—It's Up to You)

And of course, my favorite:

- This Life Has Been a Test (Had This Been an *Actual* Life, You Would Have Been Given Instructions on Where to Go and What to Do)

As you can see, as funny as many of these are, each has been selected to reinforce (or to poke fun at) a key message from *Road*

Rules®. The real road test is determined when you decide to adopt some of the lessons from this book as part of your own driving manifesto.

I will leave you—for now—with one of my favorite driving lyrics written Don Henley in *The Boys of Summer*:

> *"Out on the road today I saw a "Deadhead" sticker on a Cadillac.*
> *A little voice inside my head said, 'Don't look back. You can never look back.'*
> *I thought I knew what love was, what did I know?*
> *Those days are gone forever, I should just let them go but*
> *I can see you, your brown skin shining in the sun,*
> *you got that top pulled down and that radio on, baby.*
> *And I can tell you my love for you will still be strong*
> *long after the boys of summer have gone."*